JOHN BOOTH was born in England in 1936. He was educated at Cadley School, Preston Grammar School and Rutherford College. He has worked as a freelance journalist for many years, contributing features and articles on food and wine to various newspapers, including the *Guardian*, the *Daily Telegraph* and *The Times*. He has published numerous books, including *Vivaldi: His Life and Times* (1985), *European Wines* (1986), *The Real Pub Guide* (1988) and *Jack Yeats: A Vision of Ireland* (1993). He has lived in both Italy and France, and currently lives in Lewes, East Sussex.

Session in full swing, Madden's Bar, Belfast

# A Toast to Ireland

### A CELEBRATION
#### *of*
### TRADITIONAL IRISH DRINKS

John Booth

THE
BLACKSTAFF
PRESS

Grateful acknowledgement is made to Beamish and Crawford, Guy Booth, Bord Fáilte, Cooley distillery, J.M. Dent and Sons, Dermot Donohue, Dermott Dunbar, Guinness Museum, John Harrison Photography, Christopher Hill Photographic, Linen Hall Library, Locke's distillery, Kenneth McNally, R.T. Mills, Murphy Brewery Ireland, Terry Murphy Photography, National Library of Ireland, National Museum of Ireland, O'Brien Press, Old Bushmills distillery, John Sheehan Photography, Paula Toman, Ulster Museum, Waterford Crystal and Anne Yeats, who provided visual material for this book.

The publishers have made every effort to trace and acknowledge copyright holders. We apologise for any omissions in the above list and we will welcome additions or amendments to it for inclusion in any reprint edition.

First published in 1995 by
The Blackstaff Press
3 Galway Park, Dundonald, Belfast BT16 0AN, Northern Ireland

© John Booth, 1995

Typeset by Tony Moreau

Printed in Ireland by ColourBooks Limited

A CIP catalogue record for this book
is available from the British Library

ISBN 0-85640-536-1

# CONTENTS

Courtesy of Irish Distillers Group

# ACKNOWLEDGEMENTS

Many people, most of them unknown to me by name, have been of great assistance in the researching of this book, and I am glad to take this opportunity of thanking them: they are the hospitable, anonymous friends I met at bars and pubs in Ireland.

Others I do know and thank sincerely for their kindness and hospitality. They include: Guy Booth, who provided some of the line drawings; John Clement Ryan of Irish Distillers Group; Paul Walsh, Curator of the Guinness Hopstore, Dublin; Vincent Giltinan of Murphy Brewery Ireland, Cork; Bernie Amberson of Beamish and Crawford, Cork, and a group of the company's pensioners; Waterford Crystal, Waterford; Stena Sealink for use of their excellent ferry service between Ireland and Britain. If some names that should have been included here have been omitted, this should be attributed to Irish hospitality rather than ingratitude.

KENNETH McNALLY

Pub, Aran Islands,
by Jack B. Yeats.
Courtesy of Anne Yeats

# INTRODUCTION

The purpose of this book is to celebrate the unique charms of the drinks of Ireland, to raise a glass to the beverages that have satisfied the thirst and sharpened the wit of generations of Irishmen and Irishwomen. In doing so, it is essential to look at the wider story of Irish drink, beyond the market-place and the mechanics of distilling and brewing to the historical and cultural influences that have played a part in this aspect of Irish life.

The taste of Irish whiskey is gentle and subtle. Taste and smell stir memories of lush green fields, mist-shrouded hills, huge, rain-washed skies. A distillation of Irish barley and pure Irish water, it is the essence of Ireland.

Courtesy of Irish Distillers Group

There is much more to the differences between Scotch whisky and Irish whiskey than the spelling. The Irish claim – a little grandly, as is the way with Irish claims – that they were masters of the art of distilling long before their neighbours to the northeast, arguing that the knowledge was brought to Ireland more than a thousand years ago from the Middle East. Though this is probably true, there is no documentary evidence for this claim, nor is there for the actual discovery of the distilling process. Aristotle refers to it in the fourth century BC, and distilling was used extensively by Arab physicians in the twelfth and thirteenth centuries AD. The Irish have much stronger grounds for their claim that the

Torc waterfall, Killarney,
County Kerry
R. T. MILLS

1

makers of brandy owe a debt of gratitude to them because the secrets of distilling were carried, via Scotland, to France by Irish missionaries. They point to the similarities of the names of the spirits made in the two countries – *uisce beatha*, distilled from barley, in Irish and *eau de vie*, distilled from wine, in French – both of which mean 'water of life'.

The principal difference between Irish and Scotch is that Irish whiskey is distilled three times, whilst Scotch is usually distilled twice. Irish whiskey is given longer to mature than many Scotches: most of it is aged for at least five years, some for as many as twelve. The result is a distinctive spirit with a delicate but tingling flavour and an intriguingly herby, even mossy, smell that is quite unlike the peaty pungency of many Scotch whiskies.

Although they are nothing like so dramatic as the differences between Irish and Scotch, subtle variations of character do exist between Irish whiskies. These

Unloading casks of Guinness at Dublin's dockside.
Courtesy of Guinness Museum

differences – perhaps *nuances* is a better word – are slight but real, rather on the scale of the differences that exist between the classified crus of a French wine region such as Burgundy or Saint Émilion. Bushmills, for example, the oldest licensed distillery in the world,

BORD FÁILTE

River Liffey, Dublin

whose licence to distil dates from 1608, has a powerful presence with a certain cragginess that seems to carry echoes of its location on the northern coast of Ireland, in sight of that fantastic geological phenomenon the Giant's Causeway. John Jameson, on the other hand, originally distilled in Dublin, has a softer, more urbane personality, with an underlying note of gaiety that is typical of the citizens of Dublin. Paddy, the whiskey of Munster, is as beguiling as the green countryside in which it was first made.

Ireland has a long tradition of the making of *poitín*, or illicit whiskey. Taxation of distilled liquors was first begun in Ireland in the seventeenth century, as were efforts to evade such costs, and by the eighteenth century the making of *poitín* had become an important, although illegal, part of the income of the rural poor. This despite the efforts of the British government to stamp out the practice. The clashes between the *poitín* men and the law have become part of Irish folklore. The present-day authorities are still opposed to the making of *poitín*, of course, but it still goes on, it is said, in the misty corners of rural Ireland where a bargain is not truly sealed until a drop of the 'good stuff' has been shared.

Of all Irish drinks, the black wine of Ireland is the most celebrated. Guinness is a legend among drinks, black as night, with a head as creamy as summer clouds; intriguingly bitter yet clean on the palate, Guinness is welcome any time of the day: with a few local oysters at lunchtime, as a pick-me-up at the end of a long day, or as the fuel for a long, spirited, Irish conversation.

R.T. MILLS

Canty's bar, Midleton, County Cork

Guinness poster by John Gilroy, 1946.
Courtesy of Guinness Museum

There is a widespread belief that Guinness reaches a miraculous peak of perfection only when brewed in Ireland. According to those who hold this opinion, Guinness made in other parts of the world is to be drunk much as a wanderer in the burning sands of the desert will thirstily gulp the brackish oasis water he or she would spurn in happier times – though the people in a position to know, the brewers who make Guinness at the sixty-four-acre site in the heart of Dublin, dismiss this belief as so much superstition.

But Guinness is not the only Irish stout. There are, too, the splendid brews Beamish and Murphy's, both from Cork, famous as the city of spires, on the hauntingly beautiful southern coast of Ireland. Both have their ardent supporters, who claim the stout of Cork to be vastly superior to that of Dublin, which they dismiss contemptuously as 'Liffey water'. Listening to the soft lilt of a Cork conversation, it is sometimes difficult to decide which has the greater effect on the local eloquence: the local stout or the Blarney Stone, which is just outside the city.

The Irish bar is the stuff of legend, just as Irish thirst is legendary. Much more than a place for drinking, the Irish pub is a social experience – part theatre, part debating chamber, part living room. Indeed, the pub often seems an extension of the home; here the generations gather, young and old, men and women and children, talking, drinking and, above all, singing – for music seems to be an essential part of Irish drinking. All this is an improvement on the essentially masculine

GUY BOOTH

Spirit grocers, Milford, County Donegal

DERMOT DONOHUE

strongholds that bars once were – and still are in some remote rural places. Pubs are as much a part of the community as the corner shop, and, indeed, in many parts of Ireland the same 'spirit grocer' establishment serves as shop and bar, with butter and eggs served in one corner and foaming glasses of stout in another. Irish bars are welcoming, inviting places, immediately comfortable, where one can take a glass and exchange the time of day, an exchange that can often grow into a discussion of such intense interest that any planned departure tends to be postponed and often abandoned.

At one time expatriate Irishmen used to gather in their adopted countries to bemoan the absence of Irish drinks and Irish pubs, adding in laments for dear old mothers and blue-eyed colleens. Such gatherings are no longer necessary – so far as drink is concerned, anyway – because Irish drinks are now available throughout the world and Irish pubs can be found in countries as far apart as Australia and Russia. At the last count there were about two hundred Irish pubs outside Ireland, with a strong representation in Europe in such countries as Estonia, Czechoslovakia, Germany, France, Spain Sweden and Italy. The enthusiasm for Ireland and things Irish has not gone unnoticed by Irish businessmen. Guinness, for example, has set up a special organisation to advise foreigners on how to create the authentic Irish pub, from design and staff to food and music, not forgetting, of course, that vital ingredient – draught Guinness.

This book is dedicated to the pubs of Ireland and the people who make them what they are. I toast them in gratitude for enjoyment shared and in admiration for the way the tradition of hospitality has been so well preserved. In doing so, I choose Irish whiskey to make my salute, not from indifference towards Irish stout but because the Irish spirit measure is typically generous – 35 millilitres as against 28 millilitres in Scotland and a miserly 23 millilitres in England and Wales.

Traditional musicians, Clonmel, County Tipperary

BORD FÁILTE

# 1

## NATIONAL DRINKS
## AND
## NATIONAL CHARACTER

*Health and long life to you*
*Land without rent to you*
*The woman or man of your choice to you*
*A child every year to you*
*And may you be half an hour in heaven*
*Before the devil knows you're dead.*

CLASSIC IRISH TOAST

What a nation drinks can be as crucial in forming the national character as its diet, sport or any other activity in which it engages. The Englishman's traditional preference for long evenings spent drinking pints of warm beer surely contributes to his stolid, ruminative character. The flamboyance of the French clearly owes much to the heady delights of claret, burgundy or champagne, as does the fiery nature of the Balkan to the inflammatory effects of his native slivovitza. Anyone who has spent any time in the endlessly flat landscape of the Netherlands will understand why the Dutch were driven to devise such an efficient method of attaining oblivion as gin,

County Donegal
DERMOT DONOHUE

7

County Donegal  just as it is easy to appreciate why the proud Highland Scot, wrapped in the mists of his native heath, was inspired to develop a potion with the liberating power of malt whisky.

As it happens, Ireland does not have one single national drink but is in the happy position of having two – stout and whiskey – which may be said to represent the two aspects of the Irish national character: the spirited, poetic, inspirational vein and the darker, more contemplative depths of the Celtic soul.

The history of drink has a particular place in the history of Ireland. It is, in a very special sense, part of the culture of the nation, part of Ireland's famous tradition of hospitality, which has been remarked upon by generations of visitors. This welcoming attitude to the stranger was not simply an expression of goodwill on the part of the indigenous people but was considered necessary to the proper conduct of

*An Irish Lord Feasting in the Open Air*
from *Image of Irelande*
by John Derricke, 1581

society in old Ireland. The Brehon laws of Gaelic Ireland reflected a highly regulated society with a complex web of rules influencing every aspect of life, and placing particular stress on the importance of hospitality. Brehon society was subtle, refined and remarkable for its respect for learning; the poet was honoured as much as the chief. John Feehan described it in this way in his book *Laois, an Environmental History*: 'The Brehon laws had a well-defined code of hospitality, under which hostels were maintained not only for the free lodging and entertainment of such civil servants as chiefs, brehons, clerics or poets, but of any traveller who required food and shelter.'

Historians agree that the influence of the Brehon culture continued to be significant under English rule, and represented a fundamental difference between the Irish people and those who oppressed them. Another modern historian, R.F. Foster, has written that the Brehon laws 'were practised by a hereditary caste of jurists, a concept that infuriated professionally minded English observers. With their archaic divinations of pragmatic principles and their complex system of fines, the Brehon laws imposed a powerful obstacle to the spread of English law: they sustained an underground existence even in post-Elizabethan times and represented an intuitive, archaic and subtle pattern of life' (*Modern Ireland 1600–1972*). This ancient subterranean culture continued to affect the development of the Irish nation, preserving a native culture throughout centuries of foreign domination and affecting the Irish national identity even in modern times.

The traditional drinks of the country were beer for the common folk and mead for the nobles. The Brehon laws had strict rules on the art of beekeeping, the main purpose of which was to provide honey for fermentation into mead (although an anonymous ninth-century poet writes of 'brewing the mead from the sweet hazel nuts').

Brewing has a long history in Ireland and a kind of beer was certainly made in the Bronze Age; the great

Bronze Age pottery beaker from Lough Gur, County Limerick

Barley, hops and yeast for brewing Guinness.
Courtesy of Guinness Museum

Smithwick's brewery,
St Francis's Abbey, County Kilkenny.
Courtesy of Guinness Museum

bronze cauldrons in which it was brewed and the decorated pottery beakers from which it was quaffed have been found in many archaeological sites. In Gaelic society, beer was made from fermented barley and boiled with aromatic herbs in vats of oak. It was evidently widely enjoyed, so much so that a Brehon edict on the permissible amount to be drunk was deemed necessary: 'A layman may drink six pints with his dinner but a monk may drink only three pints. This is so he will not be intoxicated when prayer time arrives.'

An early and tragic reference to brewing derives from the Norman town of Leys, in County Laois, 1297: 'Elena, daughter of Barth Son of Henry, a young child, fell into a pot of hot malt, and was scalded and died.' Another early reference is from Rathdowney, also in County Laois, which has a long tradition of brewing; there are records of tolls of ales and wines there as early as 1276. The same town later had a famous Irish brewery, Robert Perry and Son, well-known for its Ossory Ales 'brewed from the celebrated Castletown and Ossory Natural Springs'. The brewery was proud to announce it used only Irish barley in its brewing process and was even more proud of its royal warrant 'by appointment to Queen Victoria'. The brewery flourished for many years and closed only in 1966.

A link with the early days of brewing survives in Smithwick's brewery, now owned by Guinness. Smithwick's beer is still brewed at Kilkenny in the southeast of Ireland in what is claimed to be Ireland's oldest brewery, on the site of a Franciscan monastery where the holy brothers produced fine ales in the fourteenth century. The monks of Ireland were the custodians of the tradition of brewing, and developed it into a skilled craft; they had the highest authority for doing so as Saint Patrick himself took his own brewer, a priest called Mescan, on his travels through Ireland in the fifth century.

General principles were drawn up by monastic brewers such as 'ale should not be drunk under v days olde' and 'new ale is unholesome for all men', observations that are as true today as when they were first made.

Beer played an important part in the life of medieval monasteries, where a monk's daily ration could be as much as a gallon a day (which probably explains why medieval monks are so often described as merry). Nevertheless, excess (a subjective judgement, evidently) was frowned upon, and it was ruled that 'If any monk through drinking too freely gets thick of speech so that he cannot join in the psalms, he is to be deprived of his supper.'

During the latter part of the Middle Ages brewing was one of the duties of women. The alewives of sixteenth-century Dublin were famous, or notorious, for the quality of their product. A visitor to the city wrote in the early seventeenth century: 'Any woman, if her credit will serve to borrow a pan, and to buy but a measure of mault in the market, sets up brewing.' The term 'local' is thought to have been coined during their period of activity. If a woman brewed a beer that was better than her neighbours' beer, her house became a popular meeting place in the locality – hence, the 'local'. The power of the alewives gradually declined as brewing began to be done by men, who had, perhaps, seen the success the women had made of the job.

Local beers were brewed in towns and cities throughout Ireland for years, providing both a market for home-grown barley and local employment. But eventually a number of factors, including improvements to the roads, led to the centralisation of what little industry there was in Ireland, including brewing, in the major cities, a pattern also seen in England.

It seems likely that the beer from local breweries was enjoyed by the townspeople rather than the rural peasants, who usually had no cash income. In any event, even if a peasant had the means to pay, beer was virtually unknown in rural Ireland, where *poitín* was the available alcoholic drink.

By the eighteenth century – when such famous and still-flourishing names as Guinness and Beamish began brewing – beer making was developing into one of the major industries of the country. But the industry suffered from trade restrictions imposed by England at the time of the dreaded Penal Laws at the close of the seventeenth century, a period accurately defined by the scholar R.N. Salaman as an 'incredible drama of spite and imbecility'. The Irish industry was severely impaired by the simple device of banning imports of all foreign hops, except from England. By virtue of their monopoly, English suppliers were now able to charge more for their hops. At the same time, higher duty was levied on Irish beer exported to England, while English beer in Ireland benefited from lower duty. Almost a century was to pass before the freeing of Irish trade at the end of the eighteenth century removed these disadvantages and reinvigorated the brewing industry, which began to expand rapidly. Strong competition from English beers continued, however, and another form of

*Hop Picking in Kent*
by C. Hart, 1874.
Courtesy of Guinness Museum

competition was a cheap and plentiful supply of spirits – *poitín* – distilled by people in their homes.

The art of distilling had been well known in Ireland for centuries and is thought to have reached the country from the Middle East between the fourth and sixth centuries, probably by way of the many peripatetic Irish missionaries. No doubt the distilled spirit of barley was first introduced for its medicinal qualities but it was eventually appreciated for its other properties by some unsung enterprising soul. As with the brewing of beer, the mysteries of distillation were first mastered in the monasteries. But it gradually became a peasant activity; indeed, for some poor people selling *poitín* became an important part of making a living.

An early pot still

There is mixed evidence about the extent and frequency of spirit drinking among the Irish people in medieval times but it appears certain that it gradually increased until it was widespread by the eighteenth century. One observer in the sixteenth century wrote that Irish whiskey was not much drunk by the poor or by Irish soldiers, buttermilk and water being the main drinks. A writer in 1588, at the time of the Spanish Armada, describing the diet of the Irish commented: 'They drink sour milk for they have no other drink; they don't drink water, although it is the best in the world.'

On the other hand there are many reports of the extensive and excessive use of whiskey, which are convincing, given the climate and conditions of the country. It is not difficult to imagine the English soldiery, especially during the bloody battles of the Elizabethan period, taking to the local spirit, much as they took to the spirits of other countries in other campaigns. A traveller in 1620 wrote of the English officers in County Down enjoying the fruits of the country, including the local, much-praised whiskey, along with stuffed geese, venison and game pies and tarts of marrow and plum. The name 'whiskey' is a result of an attempt by the English to grapple with the pronunciation of

Detail from *Return of the English Force* from *Image of Irelande* by John Derricke, 1581

the Irish name for the drink, *uisce beatha*, pronounced 'ish'ke-ba'ha', which was gradually moulded into a sound the English could master.

Arthur Young, the English agriculturist, painted a vivid picture of the simple life of the Irish peasant as he saw it during his travels in Ireland in the eighteenth century:

> Mark the Irishman's potato bowl placed on the floor, the whole family upon their hams around it, devouring a quantity almost incredible, the beggar seating himself to it with a hearty welcome, the pig taking his share as readily as the wife, the cocks, hens, turkeys, geese, the cur, the cat and perhaps the cow – and all partaking of the same dish. No man can often have been a witness of it without being convinced of the plenty, and I will add the cheerfulness, that attends it.

James Carr, a gentleman of Devon travelling in Ireland around the time of the Union of 1801, was one of many who remarked on the hospitable nature of Irish society, and particularly of the poor: 'The neighbour or the stranger finds every man's door

open, and to walk in without ceremony at meal time and to partake of his bowl of potatoes, is always sure to give pleasure to everyone in the house.'

The cheerful, outgoing character of the poor was remarkable given the dreadful conditions in which they lived. The peasants had no rights of tenure, their rents could be raised at any time without consultation, and they could be evicted at any time

the landlord chose. The land they worked was in all probability owned by an absentee landlord living in England and leaving his affairs to be managed by an agent who was yet another burden on the back of the peasantry. Their way of life was the worst of any peasant class in Europe in the eighteenth century, they were without rights of property or religion, yet they retained a genial, open manner. Visiting Ireland in 1825, Sir Walter Scott wrote: 'Their natural condition is turned towards gaiety and happiness.' Even officialdom observed this characteristic, as confirmed by a report from the Census Commissioners noting 'the proverbial gaiety and lightheartedness of the peasant people'.

'They are infinitely more cheerful than anything we commonly see in England,' Arthur Young wrote admiringly. 'The circumstances which struck me most in the common Irish were, vivacity and a great eloquent volubility of speech; one would think they could take snuff and talk without tiring till Doomsday'. Young went on to say how sociable the Irish peasants were; he too remarked that their hospitality, 'be their own poverty be ever so pinching, has too much merit to be forgotten. Pleased to enjoyment with a joke, or witty repartee, they will repeat it with such expression, that the laughter will be universal.'

The peasants had a vigorous social life, and music and dancing were popular. Dancing masters travelled

The bottling hall,
J. and J. McConnell brewery,
Belfast, 1914

15

the country, often accompanied by a blind fiddler, and were paid sixpence a quarter to teach dancing. Weddings were a great opportunity for music making, as were wakes. At the end of the seventeenth century an English traveller named Dunton described a scene before an Irish funeral: 'About twenty women guzzling usquebagh or aquavitae: I enquired who they were and was told they were the mna or keening women …'

One eighteenth-century landowner recorded the custom of tenants moving a cabin with the help of music:

> The custom on such occasions is for the person who has the work to be done to hire a fiddler, upon which engagement all the neighbours joyously assemble and carry in an incredibly short time the stones and timbers upon their backs to the new site; men, women and children alternately dancing and working while daylight lasts, at the termination of which they adjourn to some dwelling where they finish the night, often prolonging the dance to the dawn of day.

Any occasion was sufficient excuse for merrymaking and men would happily walk seven miles after a day's work to take part in the festivities. There is every reason to believe that home-made whiskey enlivened these affairs greatly.

Courtesy and good manners appear to have been natural to the people, who although the popular butt of Victorian times, and relished by such magazines as *Punch*, were not the ridiculous figures they were

Dancing on the Bangor boat, County Down, 1906

made to seem. As C. Woodham-Smith argued in his seminal study *The Great Hunger*, many of Ireland's ancient families were dispossessed, their descendants left as paupers on land they had once owned, and were people who could legitimately claim the birthright of aristocrats.

The ancient nobility of Ireland was not forgotten, despite England's domination, nor did its members lose their pride. An observer in the eighteenth century encountered the great family of Connacht, in the west of Ireland, the MacDermots, one of whom bore the title Prince of Coolavin. 'He lives at Coolavin in Sligo and, though he has not above £100 a year, will not admit his children to sit in his presence.' When a group of visitors came to call on him, including Lord Kingsborough and John Ponsonby, son of the Earl of Bessborough and speaker of the Irish House of Commons, the prince ignored the English nobility and made a point of greeting the Irish in cordial terms: 'O'Hara, you are welcome. Sandford I am glad to see you . . .' To the others, he simply said, 'As to the rest of ye, come in as ye can.'

The peasant population existed almost solely on potatoes in the eighteenth and nineteenth centuries, eating an average of eight to ten pounds per day per adult person. Writing before the horrors that were to come in the famine years of 1845–49, Arthur Young found their diet to be as good as that of the English labouring classes:

> When I see the people of a country in spite of their political oppression with well-formed vigorous bodies, and their cottages swarming with children, when I see their men athletic and their women beautiful, I know not how to believe them subsisting on an unwholesome food.

He noted one benefit of Irish peasants being paid in kind rather than in cash (as was the case with their English counterparts):

> An Irishman loves whisky as well as an Englishman does strong beer, but he cannot go on a Saturday night

to the whisky house and drink out the week's support of himself, his wife and his children, not uncommon in the alehouse of the Englishman.

While this was true, it did not take into account that the Irish peasant had access to quantities of distilled spirit, perhaps made by himself or a neighbour. Moreover, since the country people were constantly meeting in each other's cabins, which were generally huddled together, for music, drinking and dancing, they hardly needed the Englishman's alehouse.

Being gregarious, the people disliked improvement schemes whereby their houses were separated. One story, quoted by Lord George Hill, tells of an agent commenting to a tenant that he was no doubt able to get on with his work much better now that his home was isolated and he was free of the temptations of talk and idling that were present in the old-style grouped-together cabins. Not a bit of it, said the tenant, because he had been put to the expense of hiring a maid simply so that his wife would have someone to talk to.

Young thoroughly approved of the attitude of the Irish towards their children, exclaiming 'vive la pomme de terre' about the effect of the potato on the fertility of men and women – his investigations in the eighteenth century showed that over a twelve-year period, nineteen out of twenty couples had a child every two years.

Another eighteenth-century traveller, David Henry, was also much impressed by this fertility and the part he assumed the potato played in it. He wrote:

> It is favourable to population, for it has been observed, that in the western parts of Ireland where it is almost the only diet of the labouring poor, it is no unusual thing to see six, seven, eight, ten and sometimes more children, the issue of one couple, starting almost naked out of a miserable cabin, upon the approach of an accidental traveller.

But even the most romantic observer would be unable to describe the eighteenth and nineteenth centuries as any kind of golden age. In the eighteenth century, in particular, drunkenness became a widespread problem at all levels of society, from the peasant in his makeshift cabin to the aristocrat in his Georgian mansion.

It may be that this tendency towards excess can be explained in part by the traditional admiration in Ireland of gargantuan feats. The mythological figures of pagan Ireland, the Tuatha Dé Danaann (people of the goddess Dana), were celebrated for their incredible eating and drinking habits. The great chieftain Dagda is described in ancient literature at his table:

> They filled for him the king's cauldron, five fists deep, into which went four-score gallons of new milk and the like quantity of meat and fat. Goats and sheep and swine were put into it, and they were all boiled together with the porridge …Then the Dagda took his ladle, and it was big enough for a man and a woman to lie in the middle of it …'Good food this,' said the Dagda.

The gods displayed huge appetites in sexual matters as well as in food and drink. Fergus, the lover of the mythic Maeve, had a penis seven fingers long and his scrotum was as large as a sack of grain. When Maeve was absent, Fergus needed seven women to satisfy his lust. Such legends inspired admiration for figures of fearlessness, and voracious appetites. Such men were celebrated by the bards of Ireland in the time of Elizabeth I, as the poet Edmund Spenser, who served as an English official in Ireland during her reign, wrote disapprovingly:

> A most notorious thief and wicked outlaw, which had lived all his time of spoyles and robberies, one of their Bards in his praise said that he was none of those idle milk-soppes that was brought up by the fire-side, but that most of his days he spent in armes and valiant enterprise.

A drinking horn and cup made in Ireland in medieval times provide further evidence of valiant drinking. The cup is made out of a solid piece of oak and is

An ivory and brass drinking horn known as the Kavanagh 'Charter Horn'

NATIONAL MUSEUM OF IRELAND

$10\frac{1}{2}$ inches in height. The horn is a massive oxhorn engraved with silver. The Gaelic inscription on the cup reads in translation: 'Kathleen the daughter of John MacGuire, chief of Fermanagh, caused me to make this, in the year of our Lord, 1493. The eyes of all wait upon you, O Lord: and you will give them meat in due season.' Whatever its causes, the eighteenth-century problem of drunkenness was not confined to Ireland; it was during this same period that Hogarth was depicting the horrifying consequences visited on the poor of London by a ready supply of cheap gin – in the early part of the century the city could truthfully be said to be awash with the drink and it was estimated that one in six houses in London was in the business of selling it.

In the Irish upper classes, duelling and drinking were rife, the former often triggered by the latter. Lord Orrery wrote in 1736 of the prodigious drinking of society:

> Drunkenness is the Touch Stone by which they try every man; and he that cannot or will not drink, has a mark set upon him. He is abus'd behind his back, he is hurt in his property, and he is persecuted as far as the power of Malice and Intemperance can go.

Arthur Young wrote contemptuously of

> ...the class of little country gentlemen; tenants, who drink their claret by means of profit rents; jobbers in farms; bucks; your fellows with round hats, edged with gold, who hunt in the day, get drunk in the evening, and fight the next morning.

The great Methodist preacher John Wesley recorded in his journal: 'The poor in Ireland in general are well behaved; all the ill breeding is among the well dressed people.'

Life for the poor people of Ireland sank to unimaginable depths during the nineteenth century, and particularly during the years of the potato famine. For many the only escape from their misery was the bottle. Their condition was not dissimilar to that of the peasants of the Andes in the

# LIGHT v.  DARKNESS.

○ WHITE SPOTS SHEW CHURCHES
AND MISSION HALLS.

• PUBLIC HOUSES.
◉ SPIRIT GROCERS.
■ DISTILLERIES.

AREA
REPRESENTED
BY MAP.

NEW CITY BOUNDARY.

"Light shineth in darkness."

"He maketh a shew of them openly."

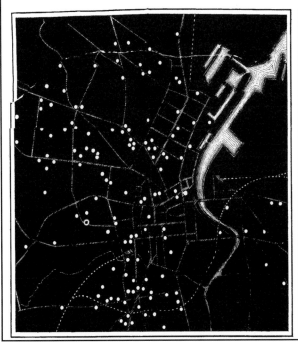

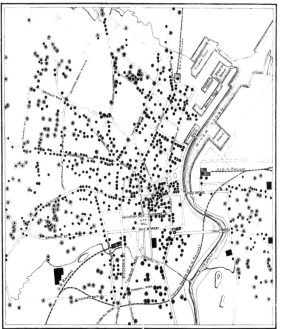

time of the conquistadores described by Redcliffe Salaman in his magisterial study *The History and Social Influence of the Potato*. Of these peasants he wrote: 'It is difficult to believe that without ... the periodical release from reality by drunkenness, the Peruvian could have endured either the horrors of the spiritual or the hardships of the material world in which he lived.' It was an observation that could just as easily have been made of the Irish peasant. Maurice Healey, the Victorian Irish lawyer and writer born in Cork, knew the miserable living conditions of many of his fellow countrymen: 'The poor wretch who lifted his heart with a tot of raw home-made whiskey and for a moment forgot his misery was not to be blamed if he acquired a habit and took to increasing the size of the dram.'

There was understandable concern about the effects of widespread drunkenness. Attempts to combat it were taken by the government of the day and, more important, by individuals who came together in the early nineteenth century to form the first temperance movements. These early reformers faced an uphill struggle for, despite a growing body of medical evidence about the damaging effects on

Maps showing the distribution of churches and public houses from *A Brighter Belfast: The Story of the Shankill Road Mission*, published in 1898

21

health of heavy drinking, many people thought it impossible for a man to both be a total abstainer and live a healthy, fulfilled life. It was not uncommon in the first half of the nineteenth century for total abstainers to have to pay extra premiums on their life insurance policies.

One of the great temperance preachers, whose name is still remembered by many Irish people, was Father Theobald Mathew (1790–1856), who in 1838 launched a national crusade advocating teetotalism with the watchword 'Ireland sober is Ireland free'. This was the same Father Mathew who subsequently saw and reported to the British government, on 7 August, 1846, some of the effects of the loss of the potato crop in Ireland.

Father Theobald Mathew
(1790–1856)

> On the 27th of last month I passed from Cork to Dublin and this doomed plant bloomed in all the luxuriance of an abundant harvest. Returning on the third instant I beheld with sorrow one wide waste of putrefying vegetation. In many places wretched people were seated on the fences of their decaying gardens, wringing their hands and wailing bitterly the destruction that had left them foodless.

Father Mathew's ten-year temperance campaign was an outstanding success. Maurice Healey recalled the achievements in his home city of Cork of the priest's campaign in helping to reduce the effects of strong drink among the poorest people. Healey himself embraced temperance as a child and remained faithful to it until his early manhood (although in later life he became a discriminating judge of wine); most of his schoolfriends also signed the pledge. Some 75,000 people were persuaded to abjure strong drink in two Dublin campaigns. The temperance rallies were splendid affairs with bands and banners and parades – 200,000 people turned out for one St Patrick's Day temperance rally in Phoenix Park, Dublin, in 1841.

Father Mathew's movement was credited with reducing the revenue the British government obtained from drink and, even more remarkably, with the government's approval. He was fêted by London society when he extended his campaign to England; in London in 1843, vast crowds watched as notables such as Lord Stanhope and the Earl of Arundel publicly promised to practise total abstinence.

The effects of the temperance movement went beyond simply persuading individuals to give up strong drink: the number of drinking establishments in Ireland in 1838 when Father Mathew began his crusade was 21,300; it had fallen to 13,000 by 1844. The aim of the campaigners was to curb the drinking of spirits rather than of beer. Indeed, beer was the temperance drink in the early part of the nineteenth century; the temperance movement had no objection to it, and government measures such as the abolition of beer duty in 1830 (although that did not apply to Ireland) were designed to encourage the drinking of beer rather than spirits. All this was responsible for the apparently contradictory position of many brewers in Ireland and England who were more than happy to be associated with the temperance movement and were often actively engaged in supporting its aims.

KENNETH MCNALLY

Crosskeys Inn, County Antrim

2

# THE HISTORY OF WHISKEY
## THE BATTLE OF POT STILL
### AND
### THE SILENT SPIRIT

*Whiskey, drink divine,*
*Why should drivellers bore us*
*With the praise of wine,*
*Whilst we've thee before us?*

ANON.

It has been claimed that whiskey has been made in Ireland for more than one thousand years, a claim that is difficult to prove or disprove as there is a total absence of written evidence confirming the existence of distilling in Ireland before the Middle Ages. This is not to say it is a claim without foundation, of course. At various times, a number of well-preserved pieces of distilling equipment, which could easily be several hundred years old, have been found in bogs, suggesting a distilling tradition of some antiquity. The absence of written evidence about distillation may not be significant and the fact that activities were not recorded does not mean they did not take place. Although often described as a land of saints and scholars, Gaelic Ireland had a largely oral tradition.

Carrauntoohil, County Kerry
R.T. MILLS

A 1936 copy of Bushmills's grant to distill, which was destroyed in the fire of 1885. Courtesy of Old Bushmills distillery

For what it is worth, the first ever recorded evidence of the making of whiskey comes from the court of King James IV of Scotland in 1494 in this item: 'To Friar John Cor, by order of the King, to make aqua vitae, VIII bolls of malt.' It has to be said that this evidence has done nothing to affect the belief, held by many patriotic Irishmen and Irishwomen, that whiskey first saw the light of day in Ireland. From there, they say, the technique of distilling was carried to the wild people of Scotland; from thence it was taken to the heathens of France by missionaries who taught the people how to make brandy by distilling the spirit from the local wine. The similar methods of distillation and the close relationship of the phrases used to describe the resulting spirit – *uisce beatha* and *eau de vie*, both of which mean 'water of life' – are cited in support of this assertion. The term 'aqua vitae', from the Latin for 'water of life', was also used in the Middle Ages to describe malt spirits and brandy.

The mysteries of distillation had been mastered by Arab physicians who used the knowledge for distilling perfumes from flowers and for medicinal purposes. Traces of their legacy can be seen in words used in modern distilling. 'Alcohol' derives from the Arabic *al-kuhl*, and 'alembic', describing a type of retort used for distillation, comes from *al-anbiq*. How the spirit came to be appreciated for its power to intoxicate rather than as a medicine is something of a mystery. The experience of alcoholic intoxication was known from the mead and beer brewed in pagan society but the difference between these sweetened, low-alcohol drinks and distilled spirit must have been remarkable.

For many centuries before commercial distilling began in Ireland, the people of Ireland made their own whiskey, developing their knowledge of distillation, and learning about the importance of ingredients such as pure water and barley. Originally, no doubt, the spirit was made for the use of one family or group, but as individuals became especially adept at the art or came to have a better site with access to superior ingredients, it became a specialised skill. This distilled spirit later became the saleable commodity *poitín*, widely distilled illicitly in the 1700s and 1800s, whose name comes from the small pot still used in distillation. The process was originally carried out by heating a pot or kettle which had a long spout in which the vaporised liquid collected before being condensed and transferred to a separate container. This method, known as pot still distillation, is used today in modern distilleries for making the finest-quality whiskey with no fundamental changes despite the much larger size of the modern operation

The principles of the use of distillation to separate liquids are simple enough. Distillation is used in the production of spirits to increase the concentration of alcohol in the liquid. Alcohol boils at a lower temperature than water, and so when a mixture of water and alcohol is heated the vapour that initially rises has a higher alcoholic content than the original liquid. This vapour is diverted and collected before being cooled, which converts it from vapour into a liquid with a higher alcoholic content than the original mixture. When the

Courtesy of Old Bushmills distillery

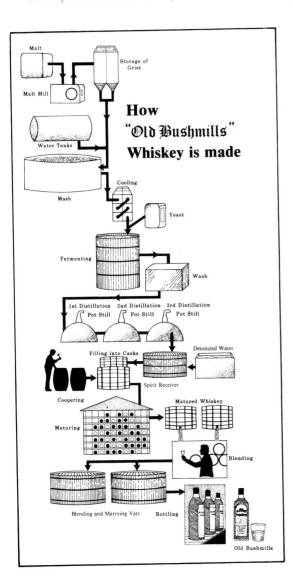

How "Old Bushmills" Whiskey is made

process is repeated there is a correspondingly higher concentration of alcohol in the resulting liquid.

The ingredients necessary for making Irish whiskey are cereals, yeast and water. For the finest pot still whiskey, only barley is used but in lesser whiskies other cereals, such as maize, can be used. In fact, distilled spirits of a kind can be made from various ingredients, including potatoes.

The treatment, or malting, of the cereal is crucially important. Malting is a process that has been known for thousands of years. Its purpose is to make the cereal begin to germinate by soaking it in water. The process is halted and the germinated cereal – or malt, as it is known – is dried in a specially heated kiln. During this period of controlled germination a substance called diastase is produced, which later in the process will be converted into fermentable sugar, and finally alcohol, by the action of yeast.

The process of making Irish whiskey begins with the grinding up of a mixture of malted and unmalted barley – the precise amount varies according to the brand of whiskey being made – into a coarse flour called grist. The grist is mixed with warm water in a large container called a mash tun. The liquid that results, known as the wort, is then cooled and piped to another container, called a washback, into which liquid yeast is introduced. The meeting of the wort and the yeast results in a dramatic turbulence as the liquid erupts into a boiling ferment. This slows as the alcohol is extracted from the sugars. After about sixty hours all the alcohol has been extracted and the liquid, now known as the wash, is ready for the key process of distillation. It is transferred to huge copper vessels, pot stills, and heated until most of the alcohol has vaporised. The vapour passes through a long coil of copper tubing called the worm, and is then

Millstones for grinding malted barley, Locke's distillery, Kilbeggan, County Westmeath.
Courtesy of Locke's distillery

condensed into liquid and transferred into a vat.

Irish whiskey is distinguished from most other spirits of the world by the use in its production of triple distillation rather than double distillation. Each distillation improves upon its predecessor, bringing greater purity, separating more of the desirable from the undesirable elements and effecting a greater concentration of alcohol and flavours.

Young whiskey is as colourless as water and fiercely harsh on the palate. Once distillation is complete, the most important ingredient in the development of the whiskey is time: the spirit is matured in oak vats for periods of five to twelve years. Unlike wine, which matures and develops in the bottle, whiskey matures only in the cask – once bottled, there is little point in storing it except for the benefit of future generations.

Wash stills, Old Bushmills distillery, County Antrim.
Courtesy of John Harrison Photography

The process by which the raw, fiery spirit changes into the smooth, rounded, mature spirit is mysterious, a miracle that takes place in the darkness of great, silent warehouses. In the nineteenth century when the great whiskey companies such as John Jameson, John Power and George Roe were operating in Dublin, the city was all but afloat on whiskey with several million gallons maturing in sherry casks below the pavements. Today's distilling operations are centred on Midleton in County Cork where the tradition continues; at least three million oak casks filled with whiskey are in store there at any one time.

In addition to the use of triple distillation, Irish pot still whiskey differs from Scotch malt whisky in that the barley used is grown in Ireland; this, the makers say, helps to give the whiskey its distinctive taste.

County Donegal

Perhaps more important in creating the character of Irish whiskey is that peat, which is used in Scottish malt drying and helps to give Scotch whisky its

Loading up with Guinness,
James Street Harbour,
Dublin, *c.* 1957.
Courtesy of Guinness Museum

unique taste, is not used in Irish malt-drying kilns.

Nowadays both countries produce splendid whiskies using virtually identical materials and with the same basic methods of production, but the results are wonderfully different. It is not a matter, however, of one being better than the other. Both are superb, and enjoying one need not prevent enjoyment of the other, just as a fondness for Mozart does not hinder appreciation of the work of Wagner, nor admiration for Renoir blind one to the genius of Cézanne.

The distinction between the two drinks in terms of their respective spellings of 'whiskey' and 'whisky' is of fairly recent origin. In the first years of the twentieth century, the term 'whiskey' seems to have been used for the distilled spirit of both countries but there was no consistency with the usage: the term 'whisky' was used by Irish distillers in the nineteenth century to describe their product. Now the two spellings are universally recognised as referring to two quite different drinks but, just to complicate matters still further, one Irish whiskey did, until recently, describe itself as 'whisky'. These subtleties would doubtless have been lost on the stalwart English soldiers who created the word in the first place in their attempts to demand

more of the local *uisce beatha*. In this book, despite anachronisms, the modern spelling has been used.

Many of the great Irish whiskey firms were established in the eighteenth century and grew into famous and respected enterprises. In the earlier part of the century the pure, unadulterated whiskey we know today and on which their fortunes were based was largely unknown except, by a curious irony, to those who had access to the product of the illicit distiller.

Courtesy of Cooley distillery

The drink widely sold in Britain and Ireland as usquebaugh was very much an adulterated spirit – indeed, the name seems to refer to redistilled liquors of various kinds to which were added spices and aromatic herbs. In D.H. Smith's *The Compleat Body of Distilling*, published in 1729, there are a number of recipes for 'usquebaugh', including one for 'fine usquebaugh' that is described as being beneficial for practically every human malady. The ingredients include proof malt spirit, molasses spirit, mace, cloves, nuts, cinnamon, coriander, saffron, raisins and dates. The method of making the drink is worthy of note:

> Charge your still with the Brandy, Mace, Cloves, Nutts, Cinnamon, Coriander, Ginger adding 5 or 6 gallons of liquor, and draw off your goods very gently and no longer than proof; and against your Still comes to work, prepare ready the English Saffron, well delivered and put into a linen cloth, and hung at the worm's end; whereby all the goods running through the Saffron (which must be oftentimes turn'd over and over) all the tincture will be extracted and run among the distilled goods. In the interim take the Raisins and Dates and stone them, and scrape the Liquorice, and slice them all very thin, and put 'em into an earthen pot, with three gallons of liquor, and covered with thick cap paper, and let to stand in a moderate oven for 5 or 6 hours; then let it stand till it be fully cold, and strain it into the goods drawn from the Still, and with liquor make up the 10 gallons wanting from the Still, dissolving your Sugar therein, and add 6 to it your goods, which when well mix'd together, must stand 8 or 10 days in a cask with a cock in it to become clear.

The nose of the head distiller is still the most important instrument for establishing quality.
Courtesy of Irish Distillers Group

In Doctor Johnson's famous dictionary, published in 1755, 'usquebaugh' is defined thus:

> It is an Irish and Erse word, which signifies the water of life. It is a compounded distilled spirit, being drawn on aromaticks: and the Irish sort is particularly distinguished for its pleasant and mild flavour. The Highland sort is somewhat hotter, and by corruption in Scotch they call it whisky.

A reference work of 1803, *The Complete Distiller* by A. Cooper, describes usquebaugh as 'a very celebrated cordial, the basis of which is saffron', and gives recipes for 'French' and 'Royal' versions of the drink, both of which use many spices.

No doubt the reason for the addition of aromatics and spices was the harshness of the original distilled spirit. The work of adding these ingredients was carried out by traders, called rectifiers, who redistilled the spirit and added various flavouring materials. These traders were middlemen between the distillers and the consumers and had considerable influence, as the Victorian writer Arthur Barnard complained: ' ... all spirits, whether manufactured in England, Scotland or Ireland, were obliged to pass through the hands of the rectifiers, who held the position of arbiters of public taste.'

Barnard dates their decline, and the birth of the successful whiskey industry that was to develop in the nineteenth century, from 1823 when new legislation was introduced that reduced the duty on whiskey by more than half in Ireland and made it possible for distillers to store their products in

Locke's distillery, Kilbeggan, County Westmeath, *c.* 1950. Courtesy of Locke's distillery

bonded warehouses before payment of duty. One of the main aims of the new legislation was to discourage illicit distilling – an Act of Parliament of 1780 had penalised small distilleries of less than 500 gallons capacity in an attempt to reduce widespread evasion of spirit duty. The result of these measures was that the number of distillers dropped dramatically. There had been almost 2,000 distilleries of varying sizes in Ireland in the eighteenth century, but by 1896 there were only 28 left, and that number was reduced further in the years that followed.

The contribution of the spirits industry to the British exchequer was considerable: in the financial year 1884–85 the duty on British spirits was about one sixth of the nation's total revenue, enough to pay for the entire navy at a time when the power of imperial Britain was at its zenith and Britannia ruled the seas of the world. The growing amount paid in excise is shown in the fact that in 1819 the sum of £17,014,000, or 31.2 per cent of the total revenue, was collected in Britain and Ireland, but the figure had risen to £38,834,000, or 27.6 per cent of the total revenue, by 1909 (the decrease in the percentage these duties comprised of the total British tax revenue was a tribute to the government's success in finding other sources of revenue). The habitual drinker was described as the 'sheet anchor' of the British constitution and it was cheerfully announced to Lord Derby in 1873 that 'we have drunk ourselves out of the American difficulty', a reference to the fact that an increase in revenue from liquor had made it possible for the government to pay off debts to the United States.

Courtesy of Cooley distillery

The fame of Irish whiskey had already been widespread for many years before these lucrative years for the government's coffers. Queen Elizabeth I is rumoured to have enjoyed a glass or two and is said to have been introduced to the taste by Sir Walter Raleigh in the days before he fell from favour. Sir Walter was certainly an enthusiast of Irish whiskey: he wrote in his diary of anchoring off County Cork on his way

to what is now Guyana to receive 'a supreme present of a 32-gallon cask of the Earl of Cork's home distilled Uisce Beatha . . . ' Peter the Great, tsar of Russia (1672–1725), declared: 'Of all wine, Irish wine is the best.' It is not known whether the Russian ruler came to develop a taste for Irish whiskey when he visited Britain or whether it was shipped direct from Ireland.

That great English connoisseur George Saintsbury is best known for his knowledge of wine but he was a learned lover of many drinks, including Irish whiskey. In his indispensable *Notes on a Cellar Book*, published in 1920, the great man recalled some of his favourite names from the world of Irish whiskey such as John and William Jameson, Roe, Power, E. and J. Burke of Dublin, Persse of Galway and well-remembered whiskies from Cork, Comber and Coleraine. He believed Irish whiskey needed to be kept longer than Scotch and said that John Jameson was seldom really good under ten years old and William Jameson at almost twenty years was one of the finest he had drunk. At its best, he mused, good quality Irish whiskey brought to his mind the line 'And the soft wings of Peace cover him round', a sentiment many lovers of good Irish whiskey would echo.

Describing the whiskey he had known in his youth in the nineteenth century, Professor Saintsbury said: 'The older whiskies were darker in colour, from being kept in sherry or madeira casks, sweeter in

Irish whiskies mature for many years in oak barrels and oloroso sherry butts.
Courtesy of Irish Distillers Group

taste and rather heavier in texture; the newer are lighter in both the first and last respect, and much drier in taste.'

It may have been these heavier and darker whiskies that led to what he called the 'scandalous suggestion' that whiskey had been known to leave Cork and return to Ireland as cognac. There is some anecdotal evidence that this did happen and it appears the deception was difficult to detect. Saintsbury admitted that even he 'whose palate is not quite unexercised in such things, [had] taken what was supposed to be brandy for Irish whiskey'.

The similarity between Irish whiskey and French brandy is confirmed by another connoisseur, the Irish lawyer and writer Maurice Healey. He described an occasion in the early years of the twentieth century when M. Hennessy of the great cognac family visited Cork and was entertained by the local citizens. Hennessy was offered a drink which he immediately identified as a Grande Champagne of his own firm but which turned out to be ten-year-old John Jameson. Healey himself had succeeded in misleading many experts in the same way by serving 30-year-old John Jameson, 21-year-old John Jameson 'from the Vice Regal Lodge', or 10-year-old John Jameson, all of which would elicit compliments on his 'cognac'.

Courtesy of Old Bushmills distillery

Many examples of the same kind of error have been documented, from a variety of sources, underlining the similarity of the two drinks. Healey even claimed to know of one Irish distillery whose total output was shipped to France. The leaders of the Irish whiskey industry would doubtless have indignantly repudiated the charge, but they would have found nothing to quarrel with in Healey's observation that none of his guests who tried his Irish whiskey ever returned to Scotch.

In the nineteenth century, Irish whiskey was much more popular in England and the world at large than Scotch whisky. When Englishmen called for whiskey at home and abroad, in America or Canada, or any of the many places on the globe where the white man's burden was dutifully carried, it was the Irish drink they wanted.

The reputation of Irish whiskey was built on the

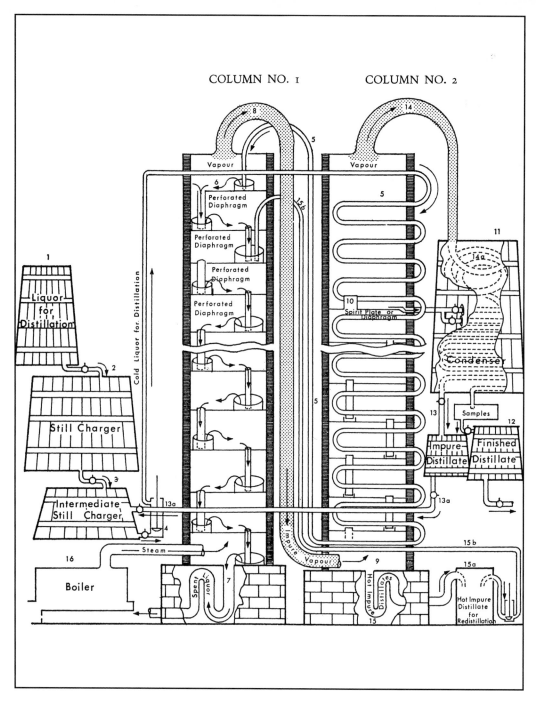

COLUMN NO. 1       COLUMN NO. 2

The labour- and time-saving
distilling apparatus patented by
Aenas Coffey in 1832

time-honoured methods of pot still distillation, which had hardly changed for centuries, and the production of a pure, unadulterated spirit distilled from Irish ingredients. In the early years of the nineteenth century the position of Irish whiskey appeared unassailable. Scotch whisky from small Highland distilleries with its strong flavour and highly individual character was very much the poor relation of the whiskey family, with Irish whiskey judged to be finer and more consistent. The great whiskey firms were justifiably proud of the quality of their products and their faith was rewarded with great commercial success. The Irish whiskey industry prospered, and its leaders became men of wealth and influence, very much in the style of the beer barons of England.

Change was on the way, however, from a rather surprising source: the inventive mind of an Irish excise man, one Aenas Coffey who was born in Dublin in about 1780. After entering the excise service in 1813, he rose rapidly and had reached the rank of Inspector General of Excise in Ireland when he decided to resign in 1824. The momentous date for the Irish whiskey industry, though, was 1832 when Coffey patented a new kind of still, the aim of which was to reduce the time and amount of labour needed to produce whiskey. His patent still was not the first of its kind but it was the most effective, and it eventually became so widely used that most modern distilling is done in the patent continuous still invented by Aenas Coffey.

The Coffey still is cheaper to run and faster to operate than the pot still as it is a continuous working unit. In modern distilleries the continuous still consists of two columns, the analyser and the rectifier, which can be up to 80 feet high. Though the method is efficient and fast, it does not give the distiller the same degree of control as the pot still method, which is why the pot still is used for premium-quality whiskey. The ingredients used in the two distillation methods also differ: in continuous still distillation, maize is the principal ingredient in the mash. The patent

Barley being delivered to John Jameson's Bow Street distillery, Dublin, c. 1920.
Courtesy of Irish Distillers Group

continuous still is essentially more efficient than the pot still but it removes many of the flavouring elements, called congenerics, contained in the mash and its product does not need ageing – when distillation is complete the spirit is as good as it will ever be. Nevertheless, the neutral flavour of the spirit produced, which is called grain whiskey, makes it a good base for blending with pot still spirit (this is what happens in the blending process). Continuous still distillation is also ideal for making neutral spirits such as gin and vodka.

There is perhaps a twist on the 'poacher turned gamekeeper' theory in the fact that Aenas Coffey ran his own distillery in Dublin after he left the excise service. He set up and perfected his own still in the distillery and later began to manufacture it and offered it to other Irish distillers. The response of his fellow countrymen was not encouraging. Some, such as John Jameson, experimented with the new distilling method but finally reported back to say they believed the whiskey produced by this method was simply not good enough. They had every reason for their conviction that the best Irish whiskey, made in the time-honoured way from Irish ingredients and appreciated by customers around the world, could never be replaced by the kind of spirit produced by the continuous still.

A cooper making 40-gallon oak casks, Locke's distillery, Kilbeggan, County Westmeath.
Courtesy of Locke's distillery

Coffey approached distillers in Scotland with his new still and found that, although there was a similar tradition of fine Scotch made from malted barley by the pot still method, the Scots were not so rooted against change. Some saw the possibilities of the new still, particularly for industrial use, and Coffey also found opportunities for his patent still in the making of gin, which was the most popular drink in England at the time.

The Irish whiskey aristocracy had turned its face against change and deplored the interest taken by their Scottish counterparts, convinced that quality would win the day. They continued to make the finest product they could and were supported by the drinkers of Ireland, who remained faithful to the great whiskies of John Jameson, John Power and others. This advantageous position was quickly threatened by the introduction into England in the early twentieth century of blended whisky from Scotland – basic patent still spirit, grain whisky, to which a certain amount of pot still spirit had been added to give the desired flavour. The new practice of blending whisky was followed energetically by some Scottish distillers and led to the eventual domination of the Scottish whisky industry in the English market. The Irish distillers were horrified by the selling as genuine whisky of what they perceived to be a demonstrably inferior spirit, and they regarded the practice as at best dubious and at worst criminal.

But soon there were suspicions of malpractice on the part of some Irish merchants who were rumoured to boost profits by adding a proportion of genuine pot still whiskey to grain whiskey. A number of Scottish entrepreneurs shipped patent still spirit to Ireland where Irish pot still whiskey was added to produce a concentration of 10 to 20 per cent by volume; the resulting blend was then exported to England as 'finest Irish pot still whiskey'. The trade was being ruined by this practice, according to one Irish newspaper:

> . . . by certain Belfast dealers and blenders who lend themselves to the mean trick of getting over Scotch silent spirit, mixing it with a small quantity of Irish pot still whiskey, blending it, as they term it, and at the end of a few weeks rushing it across to England as good old Irish pot still whiskey.

Spirit from the Coffey still was described as 'silent' spirit, the use of the contemptuous adjective intended to indicate that its origins were hidden or concealed.

Despite the Irish anxiety, the simple truth was that the English, unlike the Irish, showed a liking for the new, blended whiskey. Sales of Irish pot still whiskey fell, to the dismay and anger of the traditional distillers such as John Jameson, William Jameson, John Power and George Roe, who launched a fierce campaign in 1878 with a number of pamphlets under the banner 'Truths about Whiskey'.

Their argument was that what was being offered to the public as Irish whiskey was an inferior product that was cheaper to make and offered greater profits for the producer. The attractions of blending grain spirit with pot still whiskey were all too obvious. Patent still grain spirit could be bought for 2s.8d. a gallon while Irish pot still whiskey cost 6s. a gallon. With a little judicious blending, fat profits were there for the taking. It was claimed that most of the whiskey stored in customs bonded warehouses in Dublin and destined for export as pot still whiskey was the despised silent spirit. With these profitable possibilities, it is not surprising that Irish distillers in Belfast, Derry, Dundalk, Cork and Limerick turned to the new distillation method. Watt's distillery in Derry was one of the first to have the Coffey still installed; Coffey himself oversaw the installation.

The traditional distillers of Irish pot still whiskey were not the only people to suffer from these developments. Those who had spotted the profits to be made from blending traditional Irish pot still whiskey turned their attention to Scotland. Grain whiskey from Ireland travelled to Scotland, where it was improved with a helping of Scotch malt whisky and sold as genuine Scotch.

The demand for both whiskies, Scotch and Irish, was stimulated by a dramatic decline in the availability of brandy as the dreaded aphid phylloxera laid the vineyards of Europe to waste for almost the whole of the latter half of the nineteenth century, thus cutting off supplies of a spirit that had been hugely popular in England.

Irish Distillers, Midleton, County Cork

R. T. MILLS

The vexed question of what was whiskey and what was not naturally preoccupied the interested parties. It also became a popular issue in the newspapers and a subject for debate in the Westminster parliament. What was needed, said the pot still distillers, was a legal obligation on the part of the patent still distillers to make clear that the spirit they sold was not pure pot still spirit and was not entitled to be called whiskey. Eminent minds focused on the subject, lawyers and scientists contributed to the debate, but definitions of what precisely constituted whiskey proved difficult. A parliamentary select committee was appointed in 1890 to consider the matter in detail and in its deliberations noted that those producing the new blended whiskey claimed there was a public demand for whiskey of less marked flavour than in the past. The addition of patent still spirit not only provided a cheaper drink but also enabled more efficient blending, the select committee was told.

Spirit grocers by Jack B. Yeats.
Courtesy of Anne Yeats

The struggle between two such parties, one representing traditional craft skills and the other the greater efficiency of new technology, was to become increasingly familiar in the century ahead. Inevitably, the matter of whiskey went to the courts. A shopkeeper in north London was charged with contravening the law by selling whiskey described as 'Irish' that was not 'of the nature, substance and quality' of Irish whiskey. The magistrate found the shopkeeper guilty of the charge, to the great delight of the traditional pot still distillers, both Irish and Scotch, who saw the verdict as a vindication of their belief in the quality and authenticity of their products and as a rejection of what they considered to be the crude, *ersatz* spirit of the patent continuous still.

But the argument had not ended; a number of Scottish distillers, reputable names in the industry who recognised the commercial benefits of the patent still, challenged the decision in the Appeal Court. No clear decision emerged from this or later appeals and a Royal Commission was set up in 1908 to look at the question once again. In the painstaking manner of such bodies, it took evidence from pot still distillers, patent still distillers, chemists and all interested parties.

In 1909 the commission announced:

> Whiskey is a spirit obtained by distillation from a mash of cereal grains, saccharified by the diastase of malt; that Scotch Whiskey is whiskey, as above defined, made in Scotland, and that Irish Whiskey is whiskey, as above defined, made in Ireland.

The decision was, of course, a victory for the patent still distillers and a recognition of the role of blended whiskies. It led to a huge expansion of the Scottish distilling industry based on the blending of grain and malt whisky.

Irish distillers were not persuaded by the decision of the commission to change their production methods. They believed the discriminating drinker in the United States or England would always choose the pure Irish whiskey rather than a blend using inferior patent still spirit. Quality, the finest ingredients and the best methods of distillation would always win the day in the end, they said. Their cause was just and they had the highest of motives but they were wrong: Irish drinkers remained loyal but customers abroad proved fickle. The lighter, blended whiskies from Scotland made deep inroads into the Irish export market, especially in the United States, which had always had a great thirst for pot still Irish whiskey.

A further blow followed: the Irish whiskey industry was particularly badly hit by the introduction of Prohibition in the United States. From 1919 to 1933 the production, import and trading of alcoholic beverages were banned in the USA. The strongly entrepreneurial spirit of North America meant that there were plenty of businessmen ready to ignore the law and continue to meet the demand for Irish whiskey, but when supplies of the genuine whiskey were exhausted, American know-how was not slow to find ways to produce copies of the real thing. Unfortunately the copies were clumsy: cheap, rotgut liquor that was as phoney as the heavily Irish labels that were slapped on the bottles. The consequences were doubly unfortunate for Irish producers: they

Casks of Jameson Irish whiskey being loaded for export shipment at John Jameson's Bow Street distillery, Dublin, *c.* 1920. Courtesy of Irish Distillers Group

lost their American market because of Prohibition and acquired a reputation for making inferior whiskey because of the activities of the bootleggers.

While Prohibition was still in force, a trade war developed between Britain and Ireland following the establishment of the Irish Free State. One consequence of this commercial conflict was that Irish whiskey was denied access to its traditional markets of Britain and the British Empire, a situation the younger Scotch whisky industry was quick to exploit. Scotch whisky was much more vigorously promoted than Irish whiskey and Irish government policy did nothing to help the cause of the Irish industry. In the Second World War the Irish government decided to restrict the export of Irish whiskey so that the healthy excise revenue that came with a thriving home market could be maintained. In the UK, a different approach was taken: to increase exports of Scotch whisky and cut down the home supply so the country could benefit from a flow of welcome dollars.

The Scottish whisky industry grew enormously during and after the war, while that of Ireland shrank, particularly in the export field, which was essential for true success. The wheel had turned full circle since the great days of the nineteenth century. By 1952 exports of Irish whiskey were worth £500,000 while exports of Scotch whisky were valued at a staggering £32.5 million.

The deep conservatism of the Irish whiskey industry remained unchanged, despite its declining fortunes. The recipe remained the same: the finest Irish ingredients distilled in the traditional manner

Part of a shipment of 1,000 cases of Jameson Irish whiskey being loaded for America in 1934, following the repeal of Prohibition there.
Courtesy of Irish Distillers Group

by craftsmen to produce the inimitable combination of aroma and taste that said, quite simply, Irish. Any suggestion of moving away from total reliance on the traditional product to an increase in blending was fiercely opposed. The subject was often discussed in the Dáil but conservative views prevailed.

Not until the early 1970s were serious efforts made to produce a lighter, blended whiskey to meet modern tastes. Despite the fears of some people that the end of the world was nigh, these new whiskies quickly proved to be successful at home and abroad. By 1980, half the Irish whiskey produced was exported. The industry has continued to expand, and blended whiskey now makes up the bulk of Irish whiskey production, with the honourable exception of Bushmills Malt.

The greatest change the Irish whiskey industry had ever known came in 1966 with the formation by three of Ireland's four operating distillers of a new group called United Distillers of Ireland. This marked the acceptance by individual distillers that the survival of the industry depended upon a strong international market and that the only way of achieving this, and winning a larger share of the international market for spirits, was by joining forces. Hard and far-reaching decisions were taken following this development: the famous Dublin distilleries of John Jameson and John Power were closed and a massive new distillery was built at Midleton, County Cork, which has an annual production capacity of 7 million proof gallons of whiskey and facilities for producing gin and vodka. In 1973 the Old Bushmills distillery joined the group, which was renamed the Irish Distillers Group. The investment was great but the rewards have been substantial. From the situation of two or three decades ago when Irish whiskey was hardly known outside Ireland except as an ingredient of Irish coffee, it is now a player on the world stage. A development of great significance for the Irish whiskey industry was the successful takeover of Irish Distillers by the French giant Pernod-Ricard in 1988. Profits rose satisfactorily: from £18 million in 1988 to £36 million in 1993, and sales rose in the same period from 1.6 million cases a year to almost 2 million. Ireland is still the biggest market and Irish whiskey takes a good tranche of the North American market, but the biggest expansion has been in Europe, particularly in France and Germany.

Until recently the Irish Distillers Group has had a monopoly of the Irish whiskey business, but a new independent recently started production. The Cooley distillery near Dundalk in County Louth was set up in 1987, the brainchild of John Teeling, after nothing came of his plan to buy out Irish Distillers. Cooley acquired the brand names of John Locke and Co. of Kilbeggan (established in 1757) and Andrew A. Watt and Co. of Derry (established in 1854) and since April 1994 has been exporting to twelve European markets and the USA.

Courtesy of Cooley distillery

Locke's distillery on the River Brosna, County Westmeath. Courtesy of Locke's distillery

# 3

## THE GREAT NAMES

## OF

## IRISH WHISKEY

*Here's the health of the salmon to you –*
*A long life*
*A strong heart*
*And a wet mouth.*

IRISH DRINKING TOAST

The five great brand names that make up the Irish Distillers Group are: Old Bushmills, John Jameson, John Power, Tullamore Dew and Paddy. Each of them represents a chapter in the history of Irish distilling and each maintains its own distinctive character and tradition. Irish drinkers show great fidelity to their favoured brand, never ordering a simple 'whiskey' but always specifying the make by name: Jameson, Paddy, Tullamore Dew, or whatever the choice might be.

### OLD BUSHMILLS

The senior member of the group in terms of years, and easily the oldest licensed whiskey distillery in the world, is the Old Bushmills distillery at the village of Bushmills in County Antrim. It was first licensed in 1608, to Sir Thomas Phillips, 'to make Aquavitae etc in the County Of Colrane'. There is an even earlier reference to the making of 'aqua vitae' at Bushmills: in 1276, when it was said that the ground landlord, Sir Robert Savage, used the fiery spirit to fortify his

Giant's Causeway,
County Antrim
KENNETH MCNALLY

47

Old Bushmills distillery,
County Antrim.
Courtesy of Old Bushmills distillery

troops for battle. Each man was handed a 'mighty draught' before the fight, and the good nobleman had fowl, beef and venison in plenty killed in readiness for a banquet on their return. Some of his captains felt he was tempting providence, and pointed out that they might not be successful on the field and that the banquet might fall into other hands. Sir Robert answered these remarks in the heroic manner:

> Tush, ye be too full of envy. This world is but an inn, whereunto ye have no special interest but are only tenants at the will of the Lord. If it please Him to command us from it, as it were from our lodging, and to set other good fellows in our room, what hurt shall it be to us to leave them some meat for their suppers, let them hardly win it and wear it. If they enter our dwellings, good manners would no less than welcome them with such fare as the country breedeth and with all my heart much good may it do them.

Courtesy of Old Bushmills distillery

The noble Sir Robert was clearly an upholder of the proud Irish tradition of hospitality and, no doubt, of doughty drinking. A firm believer in the latter was the great Shane O'Neill, whose drinking habits are described in the sixteenth-century chronicles of Holinshed and who was reported to have kept in his cellars at Dundrum 200 tuns of wine as well as usquebaugh. O'Neill appears to have been a less courtly individual than Sir Robert, drinking to such excess, it was said, 'that his attendants were often obliged to bury him in the earth, chin-deep, until the heating effects of the intoxication had abated'.

Sir Thomas Phillips, granted the original licence to distil of 1608, was evidently, to put it kindly, a man with a strong entrepreneurial spirit or, to be less kind, as was a nineteenth-century writer, 'an unscrupulous and avaricious man'. He claimed some of the best land in the Bushmills locality as a reward for services to the government of the day but was careful to represent the land as poor, marshy and virtually useless. He was not to enjoy his rewards for long, however: the City of London was given the task of overseeing the development of that part of Ireland and in the reign of King James his fortunes declined. He lost all his lands (which included four townships), the market in Coleraine, ferries on the river and even his distilling licence.

The 'aqua vitae' made under Sir Thomas's name at Bushmills seems to have been well liked, to judge from the enthusiasm for it shown by a contemporary, Sir William Cockayne, who became Lord Mayor of London in 1612. It is said he was so enamoured of the drink and in such debt to the suppliers as a result that he had to sell capital to pay for his pleasures.

According to local legend, the distillery was in the hands of smugglers in 1743 but was a legitimate distillery once again by 1784, 'making about 10,000 gallons of whiskey per annum, most of which was exported to the West Indies and America'. By the middle of the nineteenth century Old Bushmills was emerging as one of the distilleries strong enough to survive in a marketplace where so many had gone out of business.

Only a short distance from the village of Bushmills, the Giant's Causeway was as considerable a tourist attraction in Victorian times as it is today. This extraordinary outcrop of columns of basalt was formed some 60 million years ago in a great volcanic upheaval; the vast, strangely uniform shapes of the

Courtesy of Old Bushmills distillery

Tasting Bushmills Millennium Malt.
Courtesy of Old Bushmills distillery

Souvenir sellers at the Giant's Causeway, County Antrim, *c.* 1895

basalt columns suggest they are the work of human intelligence, perhaps of giants as told in ancient legends. The Victorians loved the majesty and isolation of the Giant's Causeway, often pausing to refresh themselves with water from one of the nearby stalls which sold all kinds of souvenirs – and it was not unknown for the Victorian paterfamilias to indulge in something a little stronger. Alf McCreary in his engaging work on Old Bushmills, *Spirit of the Age*, quotes the story of the appearance of a John McKinlay at Bushmills Petty Sessions on 13 August, 1885. He was charged with selling real old Irish whiskey instead of water, a mistake he was quite unable to explain. He was fined £2.10s. for the offence, the second he had committed within twelve months.

Old Bushmills established a fine reputation at the end of the nineteenth century, winning medals at exhibitions in France, Britain and Ireland. The news that the company had been awarded a gold medal following a public competitive examination in Cork in 1883, according to a local newspaper, caused a great stir in the village of Bushmills and was 'made the occasion of public rejoicing, tar barrels being burnt and the flute band promenading the streets'.

Old Bushmills distillery became part of the Irish Distillers Group in 1973. Its whiskey is distilled in the village of Bushmills, as it has been for many centuries, and the water used comes, as it always has done, from a shining stream called St Columb's Rill. The stream rises some five miles away and flows to the distillery across peat and basalt, a journey that gives its water a unique quality.

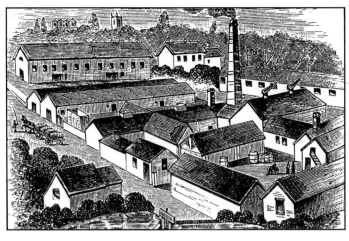

Old Bushmills distillery, rebuilt after a fire in 1885

Nowadays, the distillery produces four brands: Bushmills, Black Bush, Bushmills Malt and Bushmills 1608, a twelve-year-old whiskey available only in duty-free shops. Bushmills is the standard brand, the top-selling whiskey in Northern Ireland, which is a careful blend of pot still whiskey and lighter grain whiskey. Black Bush is a rounded, smooth premium whiskey which is made as a traditional mature single malt to which is added a small quantity of specially distilled single grain Irish whiskey, creating a superbly smooth finish. Bushmills Malt is the only Irish single malt whiskey, made from traditional ingredients including 100 per cent Irish barley, no other grains being permitted. Bushmills 1608 has the character and style that only patient maturation can give, the result of twelve years in dark storehouses where the slow process that makes a simple alcoholic spirit a great whiskey takes place. Despite their differences, all these brands have some quality in common, something linked to the nature of the place where they were made: something that has a trace of the rippling rill, of the bold, open landscape of the cliffs of Antrim, of the salt-tanged winds from the Atlantic.

KENNETH MCNALLY

Dunluce Castle on the Antrim coast

Courtesy of
Old Bushmills distillery

John Power and Sons'
distillery, John's Lane,
Dublin, 1878

### JOHN POWER

The story of John Power and Son began in 1791 when the company's distillery was founded in John's Lane, near Dublin's Western Gate, by James Power. The family was to become one of the great names in Irish whiskey, famous and influential. James Power was succeeded by his son, who became Sir John Power and High Sheriff of Dublin.

By the time the company celebrated its centenary in 1891, it was widely known at home and abroad, especially in the United States. At the World's Fair in Chicago in 1893, John Power and Son had a spectacular exhibit: an enormous model of a ninth-century Irish Round Tower made of bottles of the company's whiskey.

Visitors to the distillery in the nineteenth century were impressed by the size and scope of the operation, which produced some 900,000 gallons a year. Both the cleanliness of the operation and the quality of workmanship drew comments: the groined roofs in the huge kilns, each measuring 57 feet by 30 feet, were 'lined with wood and stained oak, like small English parish churches, in fact far superior to many we have seen', according to Barnard, and the immense still house contained five pot stills 'all kept as bright and clean as burnished gold'.

Today Power's Gold Label, which has a rounded but rich flavour, is Ireland's best-selling whiskey. The company was the first to bottle its own product, years before other Irish distilleries did the same. Until the 1930s most Irish whiskey (and Scotch, French and German wines, English beer and so on) was sold not in glass but in oak casks. These were bought by middlemen, known in Ireland as bonders, who were often publicans and who sold the whiskey – or port and sherry – direct from the cask to their customers.

Glass was notoriously expensive and only the wealthy could afford glass bottles in which to store their wines and spirits at home. In the early years of the twentieth century some wine and spirit merchants began to bottle small quantities to order for their better-off customers. The merchants then began giving their bottling a brand name which they would often register as a trade mark, a practice distillers found irritating as it was whiskey they had produced that was being sold on under the middleman's brand name. Furthermore, even when the whiskey was sold under the distiller's name the distiller had no control over its condition once it had been sold to the wine and spirits merchants or bonders. The problem was that when whiskey was matured by a bonder the end product would vary according to whether the warehouse the cask was stored in was damp or dry, warm or cool. Two identical casks of new whiskey could be delivered from the distillery on the same day to two adjoining warehouses and seven years later the whiskey in each, although mature, might taste quite different because of the different conditions in the warehouses.

Power's Gold Label became the first Irish whiskey to be bottled in 1886, the aim being to safeguard the firm's reputation by preventing contamination or variations in the product. Once in bottle the whiskey would cease the subtle and complex process of maturation and remain as it was when it left the

Power's whiskey being bottled for export to Germany, 1897.
Courtesy of Irish Distillers Group

distillery. The gold label affixed to the first whiskey bottled by John Power and Son simply announced that it was pure pot still. Customers began to order it by asking for 'the Power's with the gold label', to distinguish it from Power's White Label, which was bottled by a bonder. Eventually, the company acknowledged the customers' lead and changed the name to Gold Label.

Despite problems of quality control, bonders played a long and honourable part in the history of Irish whiskey. As late as the mid-1960s, John Power and Son had only one distillery-bottled brand, as had Cork Distilleries and John Jameson; the rest of their output was sold in cask to bonders. Moreover, many of the whiskies handled by the bonders are remembered with nostalgia today: Gilbey's Crock of Gold, Gilbey's Redbreast and Mitchell's Green Spot among them. Gilbey's Redbreast is still alive and well, in fact, made by Irish Distillers Group. At the time of writing, it is available only in Ireland but there are hopes that customers beyond Ireland's shores will be allowed to taste what is a traditional blend, a heavyweight whiskey with a glorious, complex flavour.

John Jameson and Sons' distillery at Bow Street, Dublin, 1878

### JOHN JAMESON

John Jameson is probably the best-known Irish whiskey in the world and the biggest seller internationally, a whiskey that has a light, elegant flavour. It is said to have been the favourite Irish whiskey of James Joyce, that extraordinary genius who lived far from Dublin for most of his adult life yet carried the city in his heart and re-created it with such intensity in *Ulysses* and other works. For some people, Jameson has a vivacity of personality that seems to symbolise Dublin itself.

It is a perhaps surprising fact that the first distillery-bottled John Jameson, Crested Ten, was introduced as recently as 1963. Before that all Jameson whiskey for the home market was sold direct to bonders, either as mature whiskey ready for selling from the cask or as new whiskey to be matured in the bonder's own warehouse.

Nowadays, in addition to the standard brand of John Jameson, if a Jameson whiskey can ever be called 'standard', there is the splendid twelve-year-old called John Jameson 1780. This is a liqueur blended whiskey to rank with the fine whiskies made in the nineteenth century and the beginning of the twentieth, the golden age of Irish whiskey. It was whiskey of this calibre that could persuade a member of the Hennessy family that he was drinking fine cognac.

The single most important ingredient that elevates this whiskey into something out of the ordinary is time: twelve years in specially selected oak casks, watched over by a skilled distiller who carefully monitors their progress.

When John Jameson established his distillery in Bow Street in 1780, Dublin was said to be the second

The cooperage at John Jameson's Bow Street distillery, Dublin, *c.* 1920.
Courtesy of Irish Distillers Group

city of the British empire and the seventh-largest city in the world. John Jameson was a Scot, a fact the Irish whiskey industry does not exactly trumpet to the skies, and his wife was related to the Haig whisky family (as was Earl Haig, commander-in-chief of the British forces in the First World War). Jameson was a man who believed in the simple virtues when it came to distilling whiskey – using only the finest ingredients to make the best traditional pot still whiskey, a tradition followed by the dynasty he established, which steadfastly refused to have anything to do with the despised silent spirit, or blended whiskey, which was so much easier and cheaper to produce.

Courtesy of Irish Distillers Group

Arthur Barnard, that indefatigable Victorian, visited the Jameson plant in Bow Street in the 1880s and was greatly impressed both by the distillery and by its proximity to St Michan's Church. This was the church where Handel had first played the music for his oratorio the *Messiah* on the organ. Barnard noted with fascination the bodies in the vaults which are preserved in mummified form due to the absorbent nature of the limestone foundations.

Evidence of longevity in living man was also noted by Barnard, who observed that among the three hundred men employed at the distillery there were many 'hale and hearty old men; one old veteran was over 86 years of age'; Barnard did not say, however, whether this longevity was due to hard work or to the regular imbibing of Irish whiskey. He greatly admired the distillery, which he found 'the very perfection of cleanliness'. At that time its annual output was about 1 million gallons.

BORD FAILTE

St Michan's Church, Dublin

### PADDY

Said to be the favourite whiskey of the younger generation of Irish drinkers, Paddy is a light, pleasing, companionable sort of drink, as agreeable as the Cork countryside where it is made.

The whiskey's name comes from a legendary

R. T. MILLS

Cork city on the River Lee

salesman of the Cork Distilleries Company in the 1920s, one Paddy Flaherty. For many years the Cork Distilleries Company had sold whiskies in the wood to whiskey bonders, as was the custom of the time. In the 1920s and 1930s, however, distillery-bottled Power's Gold Label began making inroads into the Munster area, which had always been Cork Distilleries' territory.

Cork Distilleries retaliated by introducing its own distillery-bottled whiskey – Cork Distilleries Company Old Irish Whiskey – although it continued, as did the other distillers, to sell most of its whiskey in cask to the bonders.

Paddy Flaherty was the man given the task of making the new whiskey known throughout the Munster area. He was a brilliant salesman and a generous man, and it was well known that anyone in the pub when he was in town had a good chance of a free drink. He succeeded in his mission so well that it was not long before publicans were ordering 'another dozen of Paddy Flaherty's whiskey' rather than using the official but long-winded title. The directors of the distillery took the hint and the name Paddy Flaherty appeared on the bottle label; it was eventually contracted to Paddy, as it is today.

For many years this whiskey had the distinction of being the only Irish whiskey that spelled its name 'whisky' on the label. As stated earlier, no one seems to know why the different spellings were adopted, and for a time, both were common in Ireland. But one explanation is that the Dublin distillers considered their product to be superior to those of

Paddy O'Flaherty, the salesman who gave his name to Paddy whiskey.
Courtesy of O'Brien Press

the provincial distillers and distinguished themselves from their country cousins by using the spelling 'whiskey', hoping the provincial houses would not use the same form. As might be expected, the distillers outside Dublin did exactly as they pleased, which in most cases was to follow the capital's example. Cork Distilleries Company, perhaps from a spirit of independence or from simple pig-headedness, decided to stick with the 'whisky' spelling, a splendid inconsistency that was not corrected until 1979 when the desire for uniformity led Paddy Whisky to fall into line with the rest of the Irish whiskey family.

Cork Distilleries Company had been formed by a merger in 1866 of five long-established distilleries in the Cork area. The site for the new group's operations was at Midleton, a historic settlement the name of which comes from its halfway position between Cork and Youghal. The buildings had been used previously for woollen manufacture and as a military barracks, and were ideal for distilling, particularly because they were in a rich grain-growing area and had a excellent supply of water from the Dungourney river.

By the 1880s the distillery's annual output was around 1 million gallons. The distillery contained all the machines and equipment the science and tech-nology of the period could provide and employed some two hundred men. It was especially notable for the world's largest pot still, which had a capacity of 33,000 gallons – it is still there although no longer in use.

## TULLAMORE DEW

While Tullamore Dew may not be the biggest-selling Irish whiskey it is possibly the best-known whiskey in Ireland because of the clever slogan with which it is associated: 'Give every man his Dew'. The slogan, which rivals those of the inspired Guinness copywriters, was the brainchild of D.E. Williams who owned and ran the distillery for sixty years from the 1900s and used his initials in a punning link with the brand name.

Tullamore Dew was first distilled at Tullamore, County Offaly, in the Irish midlands, and it is said that the whiskey – light in character, fragrant in bouquet – suggests something of the deeply green landscape of its birthplace.

Records of distilling at Tullamore go back to 1782 when the town had two distilleries, although both were small, with pot stills of less than 500 gallons capacity. Both distilleries foundered in the early 1800s, sharing the fate of many similar small distilleries at the time (see page 33). The number of distilleries in Offaly fell sharply from thirty-two in 1782 to just two in 1818.

The citizens of Tullamore did not have to wait long after the demise of the town's two distilleries for supplies of the good stuff to be restored. Another distillery opened in the 1820s and the Tullamore Distillery, which was to become famous for Tullamore Dew, was established in 1829.

It was a rather modest distillery in the early days, with an output of 22,000 gallons a year in 1832. It survived despite a number of difficulties, including the tragic years of the Famine and Father Mathew's temperance campaign. By 1886 the annual output was 270,000 gallons and some one hundred people were employed. In addition to those employed in the actual distilling, many other skilled craftsmen were involved, including millwrights, fitters, carpenters and coopers; a resident engineer was employed to oversee the workings of the engines, one of which had a power of 200 horsepower.

Barley
Courtesy of Irish Distillers Group

Hard trading times returned after the 1914–18 war and the loss of the American market because of Prohibition. Tullamore was one of many Irish distilleries that were forced to close, but it reopened in 1938 when conditions at home and abroad had improved. It was thus nicely poised to enjoy the boom years for the home market of the 1940s, but the boom was unfortunately followed by a severe recession in the 1950s when excise duty was increased sharply.

The alert owner, D.E. Williams, had been looking for a way to offset the general fall in the demand for whiskey, and found one in the whiskey-based Irish liqueur now known as Irish Mist. Romance surrounds the introduction of the liqueur, which is said to have been developed from a heather wine, a secret blend of whiskey and heather honey. This secret is claimed to have been lost to Ireland with the Flight of the Earls, the exile of the defeated Irish nobility to Europe in the seventeenth century. Shortly after the Second World War, however, an Austrian refugee is said to have arrived in Tullamore with a recipe for an ancient drink that had been in his family for generations but that was originally Irish. Following investigations, the Tullamore owners pronounced themselves convinced that the ancient drink had indeed returned to Ireland. Irish Mist was born and is widely enjoyed by people in Ireland and abroad.

### IRISH DISTILLERS GROUP

Although Irish whiskey dominated the home market in the 1950s and 1960s, it was a different matter internationally where it was all too clear that Scotch whisky was much more popular. Irish whiskey had never regained the ground it had lost in the Prohibition years and had never recovered from its self-inflicted wounds by stoutly resisting any move towards producing the lighter whiskies through blending which were proving so successful.

By 1966 there were only four operating distillery companies in Ireland: John Jameson and Son, John Power and Son, Cork Distilleries Company and the Old Bushmills distillery. In that year the first three of these companies decided to challenge the supremacy then enjoyed by Scotch whisky in the world market by joining forces as United Distillers of Ireland. In 1973 Old Bushmills joined the group, which was renamed the Irish Distillers Group. In 1988, after a fierce takeover battle between a number of suitors, the group became a wholly owned subsidiary of the Pernod-Ricard group of France.

All of the companies involved in the 1966 amalgamation had previously had their own distilleries, carefully sited near water and transport links. However, the passing of time had brought problems that had not existed when the sites had been chosen. Distilleries were usually sited on the outskirts of a town for easy access to transport but the urban growth of the nineteenth and twentieth centuries had led to distilleries being swallowed up by the towns, no

R. T. MILLS

longer on the periphery but in the centre with consequent problems for transport.

Looking to the future the new group realised the existing capacity of the different distilleries would not be great enough to achieve the targets they had set for themselves. It was decided to close most of the current operations and build a new, modern distilling complex on land next to the Old Midleton distillery. Midleton was chosen for a number of reasons: the area has been famous for whiskey for 150 years and more, it is in the centre of rich grain country, and it has a fine source of soft water from the River Dungourney. Old Bushmills, however, remained in its traditional home in County Antrim as it does to this day, producing about 1 million gallons of whiskey a year.

Midleton, County Cork

The modern distilling complex at Midleton is essentially a number of distilleries under one roof. Today, the complex incorporates the latest refinements in technology, but the major instruction to the architects and engineers involved in the project was that the character of the whiskies produced by the original companies should be preserved at all costs.

The first sod was cut in 1973 and production began at the new distillery in 1975, since which time the whole range of whiskies for which Ireland is famous, with the exception of Bushmills, has been distilled there. The grain neutral spirit for Cork Dry Gin and Huzzar Vodka is distilled at Old Midleton.

The distillery at Midleton is one of the most modern in the world, a miracle of technology, but among the glowing dials and computerised panels there is the basic, easily recognisable equipment of the traditional distiller, in particular the huge copper vessels still called pot stills, which are like kettles with long necks or spouts. At Midleton there are four of these, each with a capacity of 16,000 gallons.

What emerges from this process is spirit that is of such purity that those who take a little too much from time to time are unlikely to be troubled by hangovers; this is because it is the impurities in spirits, removed in triple distillation, that do the

Canty's Bar, Midleton,
County Cork

damage. Medical science confirms the accuracy of this observation and the personal experience of the writer of this work over quite a few years appears to corroborate medical opinion.

At the Midleton distillery the two systems of distilling, the traditional pot still and the more modern column, or Coffey, still, work side by side and can be used together. Midleton is the only distillery in the world where this is possible. The best features of both systems – the efficiency of the column still and the subtlety of the pot still – can be combined. The different styles of whiskey, combinations of various fractions and of various proportions of grain and pot still whiskey, are put into casks and sent to warehouses for many years of

maturation. By law the spirit must be matured for three years, but Irish distillers allow at least five years and sometimes, as we have seen, as long as ten or twelve years. Irish whiskey is given the name only when it has completed its period of maturity. Until then it is simply spirit.

Scrupulous care is taken with the selection of casks for maturing the spirit. Three sizes are used: sherry butts of 500 litres, hogsheads of 250 litres and American barrels of 200 litres.

The head of cooperage scours the world for suitable casks. Sherry casks from Spain are highly prized – the buyer will purchase a number, then lease them to the owners of the sherry bodegas for a couple of years, during which time they will be used for storing oloroso sherry. Only then will they go on to Ireland for use in maturing whiskey.

Other casks used include port pipes from Portugal and rum barrels from the Caribbean. These different casks have a variety of characteristics, all of which contribute to the maturing spirit and ultimately to the resulting whiskey.

About 80 per cent of casks used are American barrels that have previously held bourbon whiskey. Irish distillers prefer oak casks that have previously been used for storing spirits – bourbon or sherry, for example, leach out the stronger tannins and oak extracts leaving the wood in perfect condition for the maturing Irish whiskey.

What happens in the wood is that some of the alcohol evaporates through the porous oak of the barrel, oxygen enters in the same way and some of the natural wood extractives such as tannin and vanillin become dissolved in the spirit. It is these natural oak extractives that give mature whiskey its colour and smoothness. As a result of the steady evaporation of the spirit in hundreds of barrels, the aroma in the warehouses is wonderful, subtle, intriguing, some might say heavenly, which is an appropriate description because the alcohol that escapes in this way is known in the business as 'the angels' share'.

The casks are left for the requisite number of years in twenty-one vast warehouses at Midleton. Judgement on when they are mature is the work of the head distiller, who samples them through their period of maturation.

When he has passed judgement, the mature whiskies are sent for vatting and bottling In this process the individual whiskies are made up according to the secret formulae that makes up the distinctive character of a John Jameson or a Tullamore Dew and

Irish whiskey is matured for many years in oak barrels.
Courtesy of Irish Distillers Group

so on. Consistency of quality is the goal; because the elements used are consistently pure, the skill of the distiller enables the same levels of quality to be produced time and time again.

In Ireland this process is called 'vatting' to distinguish it from the Scottish method of 'blending' in which a whisky blender assembles thirty or forty different malt whiskies from different distilleries, blending them with grain whisky to make a blended Scotch whisky. Irish whiskey producers consider that the highest art in the making of whiskey lies in distilling rather than blending. As Irish Distillers distil and mature all the component whiskies that go to make each of the whiskies produced, they are able to retain total quality control over every part of the operation.

The most expensive whiskey made at Midleton is Midleton Very Rare: £55 a bottle at the time of writing, packed in a beautifully crafted wooden case. The making of this whiskey is the special responsibility of the head distiller, who watches over every part of the process: mashing, fermenting, distilling and maturation. Maturation is the key factor and the area in which the distiller's skill is crucial. He checks the casks frequently and selects those that show promise for Midleton Very Rare, although they might just as easily be rejected if they do not live up to their youthful charm in the years ahead. It is a long, slow process but after ten or eleven years he decides that the spirit in the casks has evolved to a point where it can be made into Midleton Very Rare, which is judged to be the pinnacle of the whiskey maker's art.

Pot still
by Robert Gibbings.
urtesy the estate of Robert Gibbings

4

THE MAKERS OF POITÍN

VILLAINS OR HEROES?

*In secret this philter was first taught to flow on,*
*Yet – 'tisn't less potent for being unlawful,*
*What, though it may taste of the smoke of that flame,*
*Which in silence extracted its virtues forbidden –*
*Fill up – there's a fire in some hearts I could name,*
*Which may work too its charm, though now lawless and hidden.*

THOMAS MOORE

The making of illicit whiskey or *poitín* has a proud
place in the folklore of Ireland, and the men
who carried out this dangerous trade, far from being
regarded as criminals, often acquired something of
the status of heroes, seen as worthy descendants of
the great warriors of Irish legend.

Apart from the natural, historical sympathy of the
Irish for those who oppose authority, there are other
grounds for seeing the people involved in the trade
as victims as much as criminals. In the earliest days of
distilling in Ireland, the spirit was made by peasants
for their own use and for the members of their
community. Distilling was simply one part of normal,
everyday life, like cutting turf or making bread.
Barley, which was one of the principal crops grown
in Ireland in the sixteenth century, was the main
ingredient used.

Domestic distilling became illicit distilling as a
consequence of taxation and licensing. Although
there had been laws governing the sale of intoxicating

liquors in England since the reign of Henry II, it was not until the seventeenth century that the English authorities began to introduce similar legislation in Ireland. The intention of the legislation was to impose order and legality on the making and selling of intoxicating liquors and the chosen method of doing so was taxation. On 25 December, 1661, it was decreed that a duty of fourpence was to be imposed on every gallon of Irish 'aqua vitae' distilled. Other measures were brought in during the same century, including laws governing places where intoxicating liquors could be sold; this was because it was feared that many had become 'receptacles for rebels and other malefactors and harbours for gamesters and other idle, disordered and unprofitable livers'.

Increases in taxation and the cost of licences led to widespread evasion. Whatever the declared intentions of successive governments of promoting order and legality, the various pieces of legislation had the effect of encouraging the practice of illicit distilling. The *poitín* men simply took to inaccessible places in the mountains, bogs and lakelands of Ireland in order to continue their trade. For many, there was little choice: distilling was their only means of making or supplementing a living in a country in which extreme poverty was the normal condition of most of the people. There may also have been an element of defiance on the part of the makers of *poitín* in resisting the authority of what many regarded as a foreign and oppressive power. Many native Irish shared this view and enjoyed relating stories about

County Donegal

Tourists drinking *poitín* with the locals, County Clare, *c.* 1890

how the forces of law and order were often outwitted by the wily *poitín* men.

The drunkenness that had become widespread in town and country by the middle of the eighteenth century was clearly linked to the misery of day-to-day life for many of the people. The country folk, much the greater part of the population, lived in squalor, dependent on the ubiquitous potato, boiled or baked and eaten with a little milk, struggling to meet rising rents imposed by absentee landlords. Some were more fortunate than others and had better landlords but most were treated as mere chattels.

In these circumstances, it is not surprising that they made the most of whatever opportunities came their way. A visitor to Fermanagh complained:

> The common people are remarkably given to thieving ... and they bring up their children to hoking potatoes, that is,

artfully raising them, taking out the best roots, and then replanting them so that the owner is perfectly deceived when he takes up his crop.

Of the poor country people of County Westmeath it was observed:

> They steal everything they can lay their hands on ...
> All sorts of iron hinges, locks, chains, locks, keys etc.
> Gates will be cut in pieces and conveyed away in many places as fast as built. Trees as big as a man's body, that would require ten men to move, gone in a night. Good stones out of a wall will be taken for a fire hearth. In short, everything, and even such as are apparently of no use to them, nor is it easy to catch them, for they never carry their stolen goods home, but to some bog hole.

The writer on this occasion was Arthur Young, the eighteenth-century English agriculturist, who was wise enough to wonder why the people behaved as they did:

> How far it is owing to the oppression of laws aimed solely at the religion of these people, how far to the conduct of the gentlemen and the farmers, and how

Children guarding the still,
Connemara, *c.* 1900

far to the mischievous disposition of the people themselves, it is impossible for a passing traveller to ascertain. I am apt to believe that a better system of law and management would have good effects. They are treated much worse than the poor in England.

He liked the people but disapproved of their liking for what he called their 'vile potations of whisky' preferring his own native beer. 'When they are encouraged, or animate themselves to hard work, it is all by whisky, which though it has a notable effect in giving perpetual motion to their tongues, can have but little of that invigorating substance which is found in strong beer or porter.'

Malted barley was the traditional and preferred ingredient for the distillation of whiskey, but the potato was a possible substitute in *poitín* making when barley was unobtainable or could not be afforded – the potato thus becoming even more indispensable to the peasantry, not only filling them up but providing some respite from their grim daily lives.

A recipe for distilling from potatoes is given by Salaman who, in the circuitous manner of so many who speak of *poitín*, explains that he obtained it from a friend, now dead, who had heard it from another person who had it from an 'exponent of the art':

The method is to expose medium size tubers to frost over several nights, cut them into slices, soak in water for 10 days with occasional stirring, strain the liquor off and add some yeast and treacle. The wash, as it is called, is allowed to ferment: after an adequate time it is distilled without being allowed to boil.

The eighteenth century and the early part of the nineteenth century were the heyday of *poitín* making, which grew as the legal industry grew. For example, the number of gallons legally distilled in Ireland in 1720 was 136,675; fifty years later production had risen to 801,174 gallons and in 1820 it was 4,636,192 gallons. But by 1806 it was calculated that of all the Irish whiskey consumed in Ireland about one third came from illicit stills. Illicit distilling was clearly more than a minor affair concerning a group of comic characters in a corner of rural Ireland. It was a booming rural industry in its own right with a thriving market and operating without the burden of paying revenue to the British government.

Fired by the need to maintain its authority and to collect the revenue it was missing, the government launched a campaign to hunt out the illicit stills, employing a virtual army of men to do so. As so often when dealing with Irish matters, the authorities at Westminster used the iron fist rather than the velvet glove. Swingeing fines were levied on towns and villages where distilling equipment was found. Fines of more than £50,000 were imposed on parishes and townlands over a seven-year period; fines of £18,000 were levied in County Donegal alone in 1814. The resentment of the population can be imagined, especially as the people being pursued did not regard themselves as criminals.

Seizure of an illicit *poitín* still, County Mayo, *c.* 1910

The excisemen had sweeping powers. There was no appeal against their decisions, no defence against their charges. When a still was found the community suffered, and suspicion and recriminations followed. Informing was encouraged by the authorities and corruption became widespread. The excisemen, who were poorly paid, were encouraged to find evidence of illicit distilling because they were paid in part from the fines imposed on offending communities. The system was corrupt, encouraging abuse, and some excisemen behaved more lawlessly than the makers of *poitín*. Planting of evidence was common and blackmail was not unknown. There were also allegations of corruption in legal distilleries: of excise officers demanding underhand payments to ignore irregularities.

At one point, the authorities offered rewards for information leading to the identification of illegal stills, an offer that was exploited to great advantage by the *poitín* men. When their distilling equipment was becoming worn, they would arrange for a so-called informer to notify officialdom and the still would be raided and destroyed. The reward was accepted with thanks and often used to buy more distilling equipment. In areas where there was co-operation between the two sides, this arrangement suited everybody, for it enabled the forces of order to be seen to be successful in carrying out their duty of locating and destroying illicit stills. The magistrates were happy to accept the evidence of a piece of distilling equipment as a sign that a still had been found and dismantled, the excise officers would be congratulated, the informer rewarded – and both parties would often enjoy a drop of the good stuff in celebration.

*Poitín* makers on trial by Jack B. Yeats. Courtesy of Anne Yeats

J.M. Synge, who brought the rural world of the west of Ireland to the attention of a wider world in his plays and books of the late nineteenth century, quoted the words of an old man from Carraroe:

Then there was another thing they had in the old times, and that was the making of poteen, for it was

a great trade at that time, and you'd see the police on their hands and knees blowing the fire with their own breath to make a drink for themselves. And then going off with the butt of an old barrel, and that was one seizure, and an old bag with a handful of malt, and that was another seizure and would satisfy the law. But now they have the worm and still and a prisoner, and there is little made in the country. At that time a man would get ten shillings a gallon, and it was a good trade for poor people.

While there was complicity in some regions between the police and the transgressors, the conflict between the two sides was often violent. The makers of *poitín* hiding in the remote corners of Ireland had the advantage of knowledge of the local terrain in outwitting their pursuers and went to great lengths to hide the nature of their operations. One excise officer spent several days following a peasant whom he suspected of being involved in illicit distilling. But every night the man suddenly disappeared into thin air at the same point – it was as if the little people were at work. However, a painstaking search of the area where the suspect had vanished revealed a trap door and a shaft which led to a large, well-equipped distillery fed by a subterranean stream. The smoke from the fire was carried from the scene by a series of tubes which were connected to the chimney of a peaceful-looking cottage some distance away. Another successful subterfuge was the concealment of a still in a working lime kiln, which disguised the distilling operation for many years. The stills were often sited on hilltops from which any approaching strangers could be seen. By the time the strangers

*What still?* by Paula Toman, based on a mural in the Falls Hotel, Ennistymon, County Clare

arrived, the still would have been dismantled and carried away – the word *poitín* also means 'little pot', referring to a small still that could be easily dismantled. The work of the excisemen and the police was made more difficult by the fact that the illicit distillers had the support of the local population, many of whom were loyal customers.

Official figures exist for the rate of dismantling of stills, but it is likely that the number of illicit stills in operation could never be accurately estimated. Most were small, like the one described by Arthur Barnard in 1830 in the mountains of the north of Ireland:

> The distillery was a very small thatched cabin, at one end of which was a large turf fire kindled on the ground, and confined by a semicircle of large stone. Resting on these stones, and over the fire, was a forty-gallon tin vessel which answered both for heating the water and as the body of the still.

The spirit produced was said to have an excellent flavour and the whole of the distilling equipment cost about £3. It was reportedly 'constructed on this cheap plan, as it holds out no inducement to informers or to excisemen'.

Some stills were much larger, more highly prized as targets by the authorities and more ruthlessly defended by the distillers. Excisemen were even kidnapped to prevent them from giving evidence in the courts. Samuel Morewood, a former excise officer, told of one such case in his *History of Inebriating Liquors* published in the early nineteenth century:

> On the approach of the Assizes in 1803, when many were about to be prosecuted for illicitly distilling, an officer, stationed at Dunfanaghy, in the county of Donegal, who was to support the informations, was suddenly seized, blindfolded, and carried away by a body of men in disguise, and brought to the island of Arran on the western coast. From thence he was conveyed to the islands of Goal, Innismay, etc., where he was closely confined, often threatened with the loss of his life, and was even obliged, by way of humiliation for his active services, to assist in the working of an illicit still ... At the end of thirteen days, when the necessity for his confinement had ceased, he was again blindfolded, taken from the island, and sent a considerable distance into the interior of the

country, where the mask was removed from his face, and he was allowed, in the solitude of the night, to make his way to his disconsolate family.

Many tales were told of the battles between the two sides. One innocent geologist accidentally discovered a large still when hunting fossils and had a chilling time persuading the *poitín* men that he was not an exciseman. One illegal distiller escaped the excisemen by hiding his *poitín* in a coffin and persuading his aged father to lie in it and play dead when the excisemen called.

The *poitín* men, or smugglers as they were also known, had many supporters not only among the poor but also among the 'respectable' classes – including those members of the bench who were known to welcome gifts of genuine 'mountain dew'.

An aristocrat, Lord Fletcher, argued the case of the peasantry strongly in 1814 at Wexford, blaming their poverty on high rents which they could not meet from the cultivation of their land and high prices which they could not pay because whatever money they had disappeared in the paying of rent. Without payment of rent they would be evicted and dispossessed of their meagre land, and land was everything to them, with the potato crop their only means of survival. In these circumstances, Lord Fletcher said, it was understandable that the peasants took to illicit distilling as a means of making money; their landlords

Eviction, 1847

knew what they were doing but turned a blind eye to the trade, pleased to see their grain being used for this purpose, knowing the money made from the trade would go towards their rents.

The position of the illicit distiller was much the same in the Highlands of Scotland. A minister in Ross-shire could have been talking of some parts of Ireland when he observed: 'Distilling is almost the only method of converting our victual into cash for the payment of rent and servants and which may in fact be called our staple commodity.'

The Reverend Edward Chichester of Donegal spoke out on behalf of the supposed sinners among his flock in a pamphlet, *Oppressions and Cruelties of Revenue Officers in Ireland*, in which he castigated 'the universal corruption and collusion of excisemen, maintained and defended by their superiors in office and tolerated by the Board of Excise'.

That profound influence on the distilling industry Aenas Coffey, wearing his hat as an exciseman, took up the cudgels on behalf of his profession. He claimed that 2 million gallons of illicit spirit were made in a single year in Ireland, much of it, he added pointedly, in Donegal where private stills operated everywhere, even to within sight of the city of Derry. The government, he said, was being defrauded of 10d. duty for each gallon. On the Inishowen peninsula, he claimed, there were an estimated eight hundred private stills which made whiskey for neighbouring counties, even exporting it to Scotland.

The energetic measures taken by the excisemen against illicit distilling eventually proved successful. Almost 20,000 illicit stills were destroyed in the years 1811–13. In 1834, 8,192 were found; in 1844, 2,574; in 1854, 1,853; and the number destroyed was down to 829 in 1884. The British government was gratified to find its efforts so successful but was no doubt aware that the industry could not be eliminated completely. It is sometimes claimed that the best of the illicit distillers of the past are the true founders of the whiskey trade because they produced pure, unadulterated spirit using the finest materials: fine Irish barley and pure Irish water.

KENNETH McNALLY

The nineteenth-century observer Arthur Barnard expressed admiration for these men, describing them as simply involved in the 'justifiable evasion' of new laws; and he added a further tribute to the great days of the making of *poitín*:

Maam Cross area of Connemara, County Galway

> No men understood better the localities that could turn out good spirit, and this fact may be seen to this day when we find many of the oldest distilleries existing upon sites which have been well-known to have been chosen by smugglers of old as places where the purest mountain streams, flowing over moss and peats, could be used to distil and produce spirits of the finest descriptions.

Evidence of the regard in which *poitín* was held is the fact that it often obtained higher prices than legal whiskey; many drinkers considered legal or 'parliamentary' whiskey to be inferior to *poitín*, which was thought to have a finer flavour and to be made of better ingredients.

Well into this century there is ample evidence of illicit distilling in the rural wilds of western Ireland, Connemara in particular. Even today, it is said, a drop of the 'mountain tae' will be tossed back to settle a deal, the sale of a horse, perhaps, in quiet corners of the country.

Modern *poitín* does not usually win the kind of praise given to the *poitín* of the past and is often described as rough, fiery rotgut. While it is not easy to obtain, there are places where a friend might know of a friend who knows a man who might know something about the stuff. Those who sample it for the first time are likely to suffer from a shortage of breath and a suspicion that this spirit would be better suited to the workings of an internal combustion engine than the digestive system of a human being. On the other hand, there are ruddy-faced men who will swallow a tot with deep appreciation. H.V. Morton had no doubt about its baleful character when sampling a drop in Kerry in the 1920s: 'like fire with smoke in it,' he decided. 'It was white in colour, it burned the throat, a crude, coarse, violent raw spirit.' One small glass gave him a stunning headache. Little wonder that he wrote: 'Potheen is a foul, stupefying drink. It can send men mad. It can put them in a trance that lasts for days. Under its influence a man can commit any crime.' Brendan Behan, a fearless drinker, agreed with Morton, describing it as 'murder'.

Clifden and the Twelve Bens, Connemara, County Galway

The best advice would be to listen to the words of these two men. On the other hand, those who dare to sample *poitín* are unlikely to be permanently damaged.

# 5

## GUINNESS

### THE

### IRISH SUCCESS STORY

*Let us find that pint of porter place
. . . Benjamin's Lea . . . and see the
foamus homeley brew, bebattled by
bottle — then put a James's Gate in my hand.*

JAMES JOYCE, *Finnegans Wake*

Guinness is one of that rare family of successful products in which the name of the manufacturer has become a synonym for the thing produced. Although some people, most of them Irish or living in Ireland, know there are other stouts, for most of the world stout is Guinness.

Although Guinness has been drunk outside Ireland for more than 150 years and can now be sampled in some 140 countries, it has never lost its national character, remaining as Irish as the harp symbol that its makers adopted in the nineteenth century. Easily the most popular drink throughout Ireland, it has special association with Dublin, where the Guinness family has been brewing since the eighteenth century. To many, the drink is quintessentially Dublin and its flavour seems to have an added dimension in that fair city. Guinness drunk there has, or seems to have, an added quality, a zest that reflects the sparkle and vivacity of that truly Irish yet cosmopolitan city, evoking the companionable hubbub of crowded pubs, the bustling life of busy streets, packed book-shops around Trinity College, tweeded ladies pottering along smart Grafton Street, pretty long-legged girls disappearing into offices housed in elegant Georgian buildings. Most of all, it reminds me of a city of great talkers and writers (which, in Ireland at least, are almost always the same thing).

As well as being the most famous stout in the world, Guinness is easily the biggest seller: more than 7 million half-pint glasses of the black stuff are downed each day around the globe. The Guinness group is a major actor on the Irish stage, spending some £200 million a year in the Republic, employing more than 2,500 people and being indirectly responsible for another 30,000 jobs – and bringing £350 million a year in excise duty and VAT to the Irish Exchequer. It owns lager and ale breweries in several places in Ireland as well as Dublin, has a 180-strong cruising fleet on the River Shannon and many other interests.

Guinness brewery, St James's Gate, Dublin. Courtesy of Guinness Museum

All this power and prestige suggests how far the family has come from the day in 1759 when Arthur Guinness, the man whose signature is certainly the best-known in Ireland, took over a small disused brewery at St James's Gate, which had been one of the ancient defences of the city and was then on the city's outskirts. The property consisted of a copper kettle, a kieve (a Dublin word for a mash tun), a mill, two malthouses, stables for 123 horses and a loft to hold 200 tons of hay. The brewery had been in existence since 1670 under various owners and with varying degrees of success. It had been closed for ten years when Arthur Guinness, then thirty-four, paid £100 down and signed a lease of £45 a year for 9,000 years, the act of a confident man.

The omens for success were not particularly pro-pitious. Dublin already had a number of brewers producing the popular drinks of the day, beer and ale, sometimes of doubtful quality. As a ballad of the day claimed of one brewery:

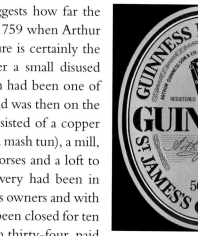

Courtesy of Guinness Museum

The beer is sour, thin, musty, weak and stale,
And worse than anything except the ale.

At the time, beer was almost unknown in rural Ireland, where whiskey, in particular *poitín* – whose production was a cottage industry in many areas – was readily available and cheap.

Like his contemporaries, Arthur Guinness brewed ale that, according to the custom of the age, was served as a mixture from a number of barrels. At this time, however, a shift away from serving mixtures of ale was occurring in Dublin: a dark beer exported from London was introduced, which was served from a single barrel. The new beer, which soon proved popular in the Irish market, was the invention of an east London brewer, Ralph Harwood, and intended to replace the popular drink of the times called 'three threads' (a mixture of pale ale, new brown ale and mature brown ale). Harwood called his beer Entire Butt as it was brewed in one large cask or butt. The new beer had all the flavour of the mixture that was so time-consuming to serve, and had a rich dark colour derived from the roasted barley used in the brewing.

The new beer became known as 'porter', some say because of its popularity among the market porters of Smithfield, Billingsgate and Covent Garden. A less likely theory of the origin of the name, but one that appeals to those who like to parade arcane oddments of knowledge, is that early brewers of the drink chalked on the barrels when they were ready to leave the brewery the Latin word *portare* (to carry).

Whatever the explanation, Irish workers agreed with the verdict of their English counterparts and the new drink grew in popularity during the last quarter of the eighteenth century. It was widely exported, to Europe and to North America, where it was apparently much enjoyed by George Washington. The success of the new beer worried many of Dublin's brewers but in the 1770s Arthur Guinness began to brew his own version of the new porter in the St James's Gate brewery, a version that found favour with his countrymen. In 1799, after some forty years in business as a brewer, Arthur Guinness, then seventy-four years old, came to a momentous

Arthur Guinness (1725–1803)
Courtesy of Guinness Museum

PORTER.

Courtesy of Guinness Museum

decision: to end the brewing of ale and concentrate all the energies of the brewery on making porter. It was a bold act but typical of the man.

Boldness was not the only quality that characterised Arthur Guinness's business dealings: his entrepreneurial daring was matched by native shrewdness. When he had signed the 9,000-year lease on the brewery in 1759 his friends thought he was mad, but the terms of the lease contained an important clause: he was guaranteed his brewing water free of charge. In brewing, in which so much water is used (both in the actual brewing process and in cleaning), this was a vital consideration.

It was not too long before the city fathers objected to his exemption from water tax; the matter became the subject of a long-standing feud between Dublin Corporation and the brewer. In 1775 the Corporation announced that it was about to take decisive action and a group of the city's representatives soon arrived with a team of labourers with the intention of filling in the watercourse from which the brewery drew its supplies. The Sheriff, a Mr Truelock, and two of the men began the task but at that moment the brewery's proprietor arrived on the scene in what might legitimately be called a 'fair

Guinness being loaded onto barges on the River Liffey, Dublin.
Courtesy of Guinness Museum

old paddy'. He seized a pickaxe from one of the workmen and defied them to proceed, it is reported, 'using very much improper language'. Faced with this opposition, the party decided to withdraw. The battle continued in the courts and was only resolved in 1784 when the brewer at last agreed to make a payment for the use of the city's water.

Water is vital for the brewing process, in terms both of the quality of the water (and soft Irish water is particularly suitable) and of its quantity – the modern brewery at St James's Gate, for example, uses 2 million gallons each day. Guinness used water from County Wicklow for almost one hundred years, until the growth of the city began to place heavy demands on the water supply. At this point the company found another supply in County Kildare. This source lasted for almost another hundred years, but in 1988 the company turned once again to the water it had used in the eighteenth century.

Luggala in the Wicklow mountains

When Arthur Guinness died in 1803 at the age of seventy-eight, his business was in excellent health, the foundations of future prosperity were firmly in place and the future of the Guinness name was secure: two of the founder's four sons took over his place at the helm. Today, approaching two hundred years later, the family remains at the helm in the person of Benjamin Guinness, the third Earl of Iveagh and the sixth direct descendant of the founder.

The decades that followed Arthur Guinness's death saw the development of a growing taste for the 'black wine' across the water, where more Guinness than any other beer was being sold by 1860. By the 1820s Guinness was being shipped to East and West Africa, the West Indies and the Far East.

The great exodus from Ireland in the nineteenth century took thousands upon thousands of Irish people to North America and Australia, and a little part of their homeland, Guinness, followed them. A franchise was granted to McMullen of New York in 1858; Speakman Bros. of Melbourne started distribution in 1869.

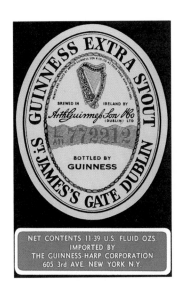

Guinness seems to have had a reputation for having beneficial qualities long before it was linked to goodness in its famous advertising slogans. An officer of the Duke of Wellington who was wounded during the Battle of Waterloo made one of the first unsolicited testimonials about Guinness's restorative powers. He wrote in his diary:

> When I was sufficiently recovered to be permitted to take nourishment, I felt the most extraordinary desire for a glass of Guinness . . . I am confident that it contributed more than anything else to my recovery.

The business boomed during the Napoleonic Wars but brewing was hit by a postwar recession, as was the rest of the British economy. Arthur Guinness the second (the phrase sounds regal, appropriate in a family that rules an empire of brewing) introduced a superior kind of Guinness, Extra Superior Porter, brewed from a new recipe with only the finest materials, with more hops and with a longer life and more consistent quality than anything that had gone before. At the time, many brewers were desperately trying to reduce costs in order to stay in business, but Arthur's decision to spend more on the product proved the right one: his brewery survived while many others went under. Indeed, by 1833 Guinness was the biggest brewery in Ireland.

The place of Guinness in the marketplace was changing. From being a drink for the working man, the eponymous porters, it was becoming accepted by

Guinness poster designed by Ray Tooby, 1957.
Courtesy of Guinness Museum

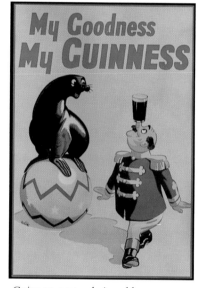

Guinness poster designed by 'Wilk', 1958.
Courtesy of Guinness Museum

The cooperage yard at St James's Gate, Dublin.
Courtesy of Guinness Museum

the middle classes. Even more august circles welcomed the drink, as the British prime minister Benjamin Disraeli recorded in a letter to his sister:

> So, after all, there was a division on the Address in Queen Victoria's first parliament – I then left the House at ten o'clock, none of us having dined. The tumult and excitement great. I dined, or rather supped, at the Carlton with a large party, of oysters, Guinness, and broiled bones and got to bed at half past twelve o'clock. This ended the most remarkable day of my life.

The word 'stout' does not seem to have been in use as a noun until the nineteenth century. It was originally used by Guinness as a description of porter, as in 'extra stout porter', referring to a porter with more body or strength. In time, the adjective 'stout' came to be used on its own and 'porter' was dropped, just as the word 'stout' was later superseded by the family name Guinness, which became a synonym for the drink.

The Great Famine was one of the factors that made trading conditions tough in the 1850s. But the mass teetotalism campaign headed by Father Mathew had little impact on Irish brewers (see Chapter 1) and Guinness was better able to weather the storm than some because of its export market. In fact, Guinness's output trebled between the 1820s and the 1860s to 125,000 hogsheads and was to rise to about 2 million hogsheads by the first decade of the twentieth century.

Guinness was now a household name throughout Britain and Ireland. It appears in the work of Dickens (in *Pickwick Papers* Sam Weller is shown in a drawing by Phiz composing a valentine beneath an early advertisement for the stout), in Trollope and in Thackeray. The drink continued to enjoy a reputation for wholesomeness, was widely approved for its medicinal properties, and began to be recommended to nursing mothers. The Scottish writer Robert Louis Stevenson (1850–94), the

*What the Dickens?*
by Phiz (Hablot Browne), 1837.
Courtesy of Guinness Museum

author of *Treasure Island* and *Dr Jekyll and Mr Hyde*, who suffered from ill-health during much of his tragically short life, evidently believed in Guinness's curative qualities. In 1893, writing from Western Samoa where he had gone for his health – taking with him supplies of Guinness – he made this report of his recovery after influenza:

> You will see from this heading that I am not dead yet, nor likely to be. Fanny ate a whole fowl for breakfast, to say nothing of a tower of hot cakes. Belle and I floored another hen betwixt the pair of us, and I shall be no sooner done with the present writing than I shall put myself outside a pint of Guinness.

Many advertisements placed by companies that bottled Guinness made much of its health-enhancing properties. A Liverpool firm, Blood, Wolfe and Co., carried a testimonial in 1906 from no less an authority than Charles Cameron MD, Vice President of the Royal College of Surgeons, Ireland, and Public Analyst for Dublin, who announced:

> I have analysed a specimen of Messrs. A. Guinness, Son & Co's Foreign Export Stout, submitted to me for that purpose by Messrs. Blood, Wolfe & Co., foreign export bottlers, Liverpool. I find it to be a perfectly pure article prepared only from malt and hops. It possesses in the highest degree the good qualities of Dublin Export Stout, and has evidently been brewed from the very best materials. It contains

Barge carrying empties from the Dublin Custom House to the jetty on Victoria Quay.
Courtesy of Guinness Museum

Inside the malt store, Guinness brewery, Dublin, 1907.
Courtesy of Guinness Museum

nearly seven per cent of solid matter in solution and is, therefore, a food as well as a stimulant and tonic.

Evidence of Guinness's long-lasting properties came in 1927 when an expedition to the South Pole discovered the base camp of Douglas Mawson, the Australian explorer who discovered the South Magnetic Pole in 1909. The expedition reported:

> The stores were in good condition after 18 years: cocoa, salt, flour and matches were found to be as good as when first placed there. There were also four bottles of Guinness on a shelf which, though frozen, were put to excellent use.

For most people outside Ireland, bottled Guinness was the only Guinness available and the reputation of the company abroad, certainly in England, was based on the dry, hoppy flavour of bottled Guinness rather than the fresh, creamy draught Guinness that is widely enjoyed today. Over the years the brewery at St James's Gate has expanded mightily, and grown from the original 4 acres described in the original lease to the present 60 acres. In the late nineteenth century the Guinness brewery was a city within a city, employing an army of men: coopers, carpenters, draymen, carters and others using a wide range of

Guinness Ireland bottling hall at Macardle's brewery, Dundalk, County Louth.
Courtesy of Guinness Museum

The final consignments of
Guinness to be transported on
the Liffey by barge,
Dublin, 1961.
Courtesy of Guinness Museum

essential skills and crafts that have long been rendered obsolete by newer technology. To give just one example: at one time mountains of wooden barrels, a quarter of a million of them, were stacked in the cooperage yard of the brewery, every one hand-made by the brewery's own coopers and repaired by them when the barrels were returned. (For much of the nineteenth century, wood was essential to the life of the brewery, used for mash tuns and storage vessels as well as for casks.) But the traditional techniques of brewing were changing with the scientific advances of the Industrial Revolution, and great machines of iron and copper and brass came to be used to produce the necessary power to operate the brewery. Nevertheless, draught horses continued to be used until the early 1960s in the delivery of Guinness in and around Dublin, the sound of their patient progress along the streets becoming part of the life of the city.

Transport, the ability to carry products to customers and to provide raw materials for the brewery's needs, was essential to the success of the Guinness enterprise. In the early days of the nineteenth century, the company used the waterways that linked Dublin through the Barrow navigational system to the rich grain areas of the southeast. The beginnings of the railway system in the 1830s helped to ease the movement of both vital raw materials and the finished product throughout Ireland.

The seaways from Dublin have been vital to the export progress of Guinness to the larger world. The company's barges were a feature of Dublin until 1961, chugging their way between the brewery and the port. James Joyce remembered the days when as one 'set foot on O'Connell Bridge a puffball of smoke plumed up from the parapet . . . brewery barge'. Generations of small boys used to scramble on the bridges and peer at the barges as they passed below, cheeking the captains with ironic cries of 'Hey, mister. Bring us back a parrot!' Steamers were used to ferry the precious cargoes to Liverpool, Manchester and Bristol; the steamers have given way in modern times to the world's first beer tanker ships, which carry Guinness to Liverpool for onward shipment to the rest of the world.

The impetus of growth led the company to go public in 1886; it was floated on the London Stock Exchange and the huge sum of £6 million was raised for 49 per cent of the equity. A great expansion of the brewery followed, with a new cooperage, racking shed, maltings, vathouses, an internal railway system, and the huge new machines to power the workings of the brewery, which by the early years of the twentieth century was the largest in the world. Science, meanwhile, was coming to the aid of the brewer with techniques to improve the quality of ingredients and to ensure high standards of quality control.

After the booming years of the First World War, the familiar cyclical pattern emerged and a period of depression followed. The introduction of Prohibition in the United States did nothing for the company's sales; nor did the clumsy efforts of bootleg brewers in copying Guinness do anything for the reputation of Irish stout.

Guinness's brilliant and innovative advertising campaigns might seem to have been an inseparable part of the company's history from the start, but it is a curious fact that the company showed little interest in publicity of this kind until well into the twentieth century. It was not until 1929 that perhaps the most

Guinness poster by John Gilroy, 1949.
Courtesy of Guinness Museum

Guinness poster by John Gilroy, 1936.
Courtesy of Guinness Museum

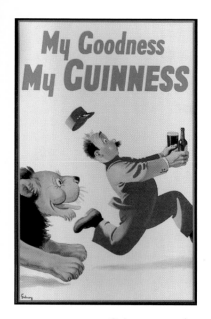

Guinness poster by
John Gilroy, 1939.
Courtesy of Guinness Museum

Adding leaf hops into the
copper, Guinness brewery,
Dublin, 1957.
Courtesy of Guinness Museum

famous of its advertising campaigns began. Guinness's first-ever advertisement for its product, which appeared on 2 February 1929, is probably the best remembered for its simple claim 'Guinness is good for you', a phrase that has passed into the language. This advertisement was followed by a series featuring an extraordinary menagerie of animals including polar bears, toucans and, above all, seals: characters that dominated advertising hoardings in cities throughout the world. The humour was simple, the message immediate: one of the best-known showed a seal balancing a glass of the dark stuff on its nose, apparently making off with it, and pursued by a frantic zoo keeper under the legend 'My goodness, my Guinness'. This brilliant series of advertisements was the work of John Gilroy, a Dublin artist, who caricatured himself as the distraught zoo keeper. 'Guinness for strength' was another great slogan and campaign, but the menagerie of animals had a special charm, brightening the day of many a man and woman travelling to and from work, spotted from buses and trains. Among the most striking of these advertisements was a drawing of a toucan with two glasses of Guinness and the ingenious, hard-to-forget rhyme:

If he can say as you can
Guinness is good for you
How grand to be a Toucan
Just think what Toucan do.

Leaf hops were still being
added by hand in the 1970s.
Courtesy of Guinness Museum

The first Guinness brewery outside Ireland was
established at Park Royal in London in 1935; today
the plant supplies most of England. Since 1962,
Guinness breweries have been built in Nigeria,

Malaysia, Cameroun and Ghana; Guinness is brewed under contract in several other places, including Canada and Australia. The company keeps a close eye on the work of these brewers and exports specially matured stout from Dublin for blending into the overseas brews to ensure their flavour is authentic. Guinness is particularly popular in Africa, where it has been available since the nineteenth century. It is brewed for local tastes, sweeter and much stronger than the Guinness made in Dublin, 10 per cent alcohol as against the 4 per cent of the Irish brew. Regular drinkers of Dublin Guinness may be surprised to learn that the Guinness brewed in Africa has a reputation as an aid to virility and was promoted locally with the slogan 'a baby in every bottle'. More than 40 per cent of Guinness stout brewed in Ireland is exported to more than 120 countries.

Vast sums of money have been spent on updating and modernising the Dublin brewery to keep pace with improved technology. In the 1980s some £120 million was invested in a new brewhouse, a new wort production plant, new fermentation and beer processing plants, new keg plants and a new research and laboratory complex.

Despite these large sums and all the technology now involved, brewing remains essentially the same process it was when Arthur Guinness carried out his own brewing in the eighteenth century. The only ingredients used are barley, hops, yeast and water. All the barley comes from Ireland and Guinness spends some £15 million a year on buying barley from about 6,000 farmers. The hops, in pellet form these days, come from England and Bavaria.

Barley, the main ingredient, becomes what is called 'malt' through a process of germination: the barley is soaked in water and germinates under controlled conditions. During this process the starch in the grain begins to be ready to be converted into sugars. Part of the barley is steam-cooked and rolled to form flakes (which help what the brewers call 'head retention' and the rest of us know as the staying power of the thick, snowy head

'Black is beautiful' – a Guinness advertisement from the 1970s.
Courtesy of Guinness Museum

Giant fermentation vessels, Guinness brewery, Dublin.
Courtesy of Guinness Museum

of a good pint). Some barley and malt is roasted, just like coffee beans, and it is this that gives Guinness its beautiful velvet dark colour. The malt, roast and flakes make up what is known as the grist, which is mashed in hot water – the water still comes from the Wicklow Mountains, close to where the Liffey rises, and has a softness and purity that are ideal for the brewing of stout. From this mashing comes a dark sweet liquid called wort which is transferred to 20-tonne giant kettles and boiled with hops. These give the Guinness its characteristic tangy flavour. After boiling and hopping, the wort is transferred to fermenting tanks where the crucial element, yeast, is added. This converts the sugars derived from the grain starch into alcohol. The kind of yeast used is critical in all brewing operations: it contributes to the essential character of the beer, and all brewers take the greatest possible pains to use a yeast that produces the desired result. At Guinness the same strain of yeast is used as in the eighteenth-century brewery; samples are kept in secure conditions to make sure the same yeast will be available for brewing operations for at least another two hundred years.

Fermentation takes about forty-eight hours and is followed by maturation and conditioning, which can take up to ten days before the ruby-dark liquid, which now thoroughly merits the name Guinness, is permitted to start its journey to appreciative drinkers all over the world.

Taking samples of wort during the brewing process, Guinness brewery, Dublin, 1957.
Courtesy of Guinness Museum

"Guinness . . . Guinness . . . Guinness!"

These days, there is more to the Guinness group than the dark wine of Ireland. Through its offshoot United Distillers, which, ironically, is best known for Scotch whiskies such as Johnny Walker, Bell's and Dewar's, as well as Gordon's gin, Guinness plc is one of the three largest drinks companies in the world. In Ireland the company produces a number of lagers, including Harp, Carlsberg, Hoffman and Satzenbrau as well as the virtually nonalcoholic lager Kaliber. Fürstenberg and Budweiser beers are brewed under licence and another Guinness company, Irish Ale Breweries, is responsible for Ireland's best-selling ale, Smithwick's, and for Macardle's. Smithwick's is brewed at Kilkenny in the country's oldest brewery, St Francis's Abbey, which dates from 1710. The Macardle Moore brewery is based at Dundalk, where it has produced ale since the nineteenth century.

### IS IRISH BEST?

That Guinness brewed in Dublin is infinitely superior to Guinness brewed anywhere else, especially England, is a truth almost universally acknowledged by lovers of what Joyce called the wine of the country. Exiled Irishmen in London bars grow tearful or even angry at the fates that have separated them from the divine brew of Dublin, just as returning expatriates see it as their first duty on coming home to the old country to down a glass of draught Dublin Guinness; the returnees can easily be

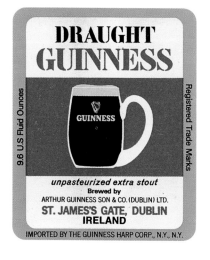

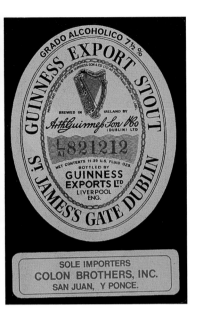

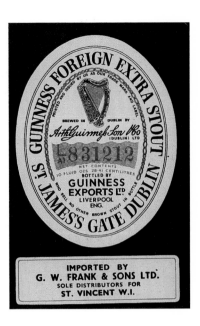

identified, even among their good-humoured fellow countrymen, by the deep, benign contentment of their countenances. Even those who are not brought up on Guinness, unfortunates from other lands who visit Ireland and who sample Irish Guinness for the first time, are frequently converted immediately to the strong body of opinion that insists that Irish Guinness is best.

Curiously, those in the best position to comment on the matter, the brewers of Guinness themselves, say these people are misguided, that there is no difference at all between the Guinness brewed in Dublin and that brewed in London's Park Royal.

The materials used – barley, water, yeast and hops – are the same, production methods are the same, and the alcoholic strength, of some 4 per cent, is the same. True, the water is not Irish water, but these days chemists are able to treat the water used in brewing and make it in chemical terms exactly as they wish it to be, so the source of the water is unimportant: water from the Thames Valley can easily be transformed into water as soft as the soft waters of County Wicklow.

Some experts at Guinness will concede that the possibility of a difference in taste exists, attributable to the way Guinness is served in the two countries. The people who serve Guinness in Ireland are highly trained and thoroughly understand the importance of drawing off nine-tenths of the stout, waiting for an interval, and then adding the remainder, topping it with a thick head. Opinions about the length of the interval vary considerably, perhaps influenced by the degree of thirst of the expectant customer. In Dublin, it is said, five minutes is usual, in the north of Ireland only a little less. But in Cork an expert claimed twenty seconds is sufficient. Some of those who handle the drink in Britain do not come from the same tradition, and they are sometimes guilty of rushing the ritual of serving, and spoiling the appearance of the stout.

There may be an element of the traditional conflict between science and faith in the popular view of the differences between Dublin and 'foreign' Guinness. It is a little like the argument about the difference

A pint of the black stuff.
Courtesy of Guinness Museum

between white and brown eggs. The food scientist assures the buying public that there is no difference in nutritional value or taste between white and brown eggs. To which the customer listens patiently and responds, 'But I prefer brown eggs.'

So, the consensus of opinion is that Guinness brewed in Dublin is best. It is not that Guinness does not travel – the company exports to 120 countries. Perhaps it is the way Guinness is served in Ireland, or it may be the engaging clamour of the pubs where it is enjoyed, or it may simply be that being in Ireland makes everything seem better, including the drink. As one seasoned Guinness imbiber observed from his accustomed corner in Dublin's Oval pub: 'I've heard of plenty of people comin' to Dublin for the Guinness but I've never heard of any man goin' to London for a pint of it.'

### LITERARY LIBATION

Guinness seems to have had an affinity with Dublin's scribblers, wordsmiths, literary men of varying levels of distinction, loosening their tongues and sharpening their wits. Among the greatest of these was James Joyce, who from his self-imposed exile on the Continent remembered the 'dull-thudding Guinness barrels' of his youth. It was also in *Ulysses* that he referred to:

> . . . the foaming ebon ale which the noble twin brothers Bungiveagh and Bungardilaun brew ever in their divine alevats . . . For they garner the succulent berries of the hop and mass and sift and bruise and brew them and they mix therewith sour juices and bring the must to the sacred fire and cease not night and day from toil, those cunning brothers, lords of the vat.

Oscar Wilde was more a frequenter of salons than saloons but his father Sir William Wilde, the great oculist, enjoyed sharing a bottle or two of Guinness with friends. Another medical man, and a man of letters, Oliver St John Gogarty, was very much a frequenter of pubs in his youth; it is said that it was he who first introduced James Joyce to the delights of Guinness – in later life, perhaps in consequence of his exile, Joyce preferred a light Swiss wine. It was Gogarty who persuaded Yeats to make his first visit to a pub, Toner's in Lower Baggot Street, Dublin. The great man entered, sipped a small sherry, mused for a moment, then rose and announced, 'I have seen a pub now. Will you kindly take me home?'

The Long Stone,
Townsend Street, Dublin

The story is entirely convincing given Yeats's patrician manner, but other pubs can claim to have enjoyed his patronage, if only briefly, such as the Cheshire Cheese in London's Fleet Street. Peter Walsh, curator of the Guinness Museum in Dublin, has done sterling and selfless work in tracking down the watering holes of the literati and his pamphlet on Dublin's pubs is a delightful guide. Sean O'Casey was a regular at Cleary's in Amiens Street, Samuel Beckett first sampled Guinness at Mooney's in Abbey Street and was a Guinness drinker to the end of his days (yet despite this agreeable habit retained his austere, nihilistic view of life). The roistering Brendan Behan was known in many of the city's pubs, particularly McDaid's in Harry Street, where Patrick Kavanagh and Brian O'Nolan were also regulars. It is to Brian O'Nolan, wearing his Flann O'Brien hat in *At Swim-Two-Birds*, that I leave the last words, the defiant call of the true Dublin drinker:

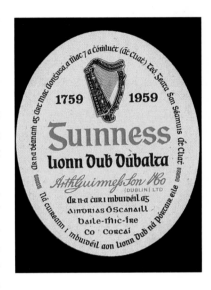

> When money's tight and is hard to get
> And your horse has also ran,
> When all you have is a heap of debt –
> A pint of plain is your only man.

GUY BOOTH

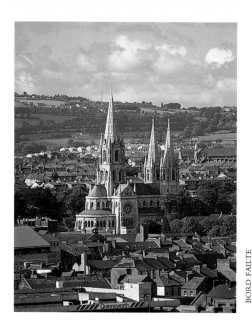

St Finbarr's Cathedral,
Cork city

BORD FAILTE

6

CORK, CITY OF SPIRES

AND

GREAT STOUTS

*On this I ponder*
*Where'er I wander,*
*And thus grow fonder*
*Sweet Cork of thee!*
*With thy bells of Shandon,*
*That sound so grand on*
*The pleasant waters*
*Of the River Lee.*

FRANCIS SYLVESTER MAHONY, 'THE BELLS OF SHANDON'

The city of Cork has many attractions. It is famously beautiful, a city of waterways, likened by some to Venice or Amsterdam. But the comparisons are misleading. Cork is proudly itself, an ancient port, a city of broad streets and bridges over the two arms of the River Lee that surround Cork, making it an island where the masts of ships rise on the quays outside City Hall.

Cork has a strong feeling of the world beyond Ireland, of the sunny, southern cities of France and Italy, a resemblance strengthened by its many bars and cafés and by the universal local habit of strolling along the main thoroughfares. These act as a kind of open-air theatre in which the people of Cork meet to debate, to philosophise, to gossip, and to dream.

Cork has another claim to greatness: it is the home of two of Ireland's greatest stouts: Beamish and Murphy's. The brewing operations are tiny when viewed beside those of Guinness, but they are nevertheless substantial, and each product has its own band of faithful and growing supporters. Each has become more widely known beyond Ireland, partly because both have come under the wing of major international companies in recent years: Beamish is part of the Australian brewing giant, Elders IXL, that is responsible for Foster's lager, and Murphy Brewery Ireland Limited is a subsidiary of Heineken International.

Beamish has a distinctive dark, slightly bitter flavour, quite different from Guinness or Murphy's. The brewers say its individuality is the

Courtesy of Beamish and Crawford

result of a number of factors: the yeast which has evolved from the yeast used in the late eighteenth century when the company was established, one other unusual raw material, and the method of fermentation. The ingredients are roasted barley, malted wheat, two kinds of hops (for aroma and for bitterness), yeast and local water. The unusual item, and the one that may do most to explain the particular style and flavour of Beamish, is

The River Lee, County Cork

malted wheat. This is not generally used by brewers as it clogs up the filters during the brewing process, but it presents no problems in the highly adaptable Beamish operation.

Beamish is easily the senior of the remaining two Cork brewers – at one time there were thirty brewers in the Cork area, nine of them in Cork city itself. Beamish and Crawford plc, to give the company its modern title, began in 1792 when William Beamish and William Crawford took over an existing brewery, which they renamed the Cork Porter Brewery. Even then the brewery had a long history, as ale had been brewed there since 1645.

At the time Messrs Beamish and Crawford went into business, porter was being shipped to Ireland from the ports of Liverpool and Bristol in large quantities – 60,000 barrels of porter were imported through Cork alone in 1792. The partners recognised porter as the drink of the future and were proved right. They are said to have sought the advice of the greatest stout brewer of them all, Arthur Guinness of Dublin, already a veteran having established his brewery more than thirty years earlier. It may be that Arthur Guinness later regretted having been so free with his advice, because Beamish and Crawford soon developed into major competitors. In 1809 a writer noted: 'Guinness is the second Brewery in Ireland, Beamish & Crawford of Cork, who brewed upwards of 100,000 barrels a year, standing first.' The brewery continued to prosper and was relatively unscathed by the great temperance campaign led by Cork's own Father Mathew between 1838 and 1848. By 1861 production at Beamish had risen to 120,000 barrels a year, and some 350 tradesmen and labourers were employed. The company remained Ireland's leading brewer until later in the nineteeth century when it finally and irrevocably lost the position to Guinness.

Today Beamish is brewed on the same site as it was more than two hundred years ago, at South Main Street in the busy heart of Cork city. The business is an appealing mix of past and present. The timbered building that is the administrative centre stands beside the high-tech apparatus of the modern brewery

Beamish and Crawford's head office in South Main Street, Cork, where the company has been doing business since 1792.
Courtesy of John Sheehan Photography

plant. Many faded documents are displayed in the panelled and galleried entrance lobby in which gleaming brass mash tun plates last used in 1880 are set into the floor. One piece of greying parchment refers to the days when the company ran its own shipping fleet to transport porter to nearby coastal villages because it was easier than by road. The document is written in the elegant copperplate handwriting of the period:

> Shipped by the grace of God in good order and well conditioned by Beamish & Crawford Brewery in and upon the good ship called the Belteron whereof its master, under God for this present voyage and now at anchor in the port of Cork and by God's grace bound for Youghall, One Hundred and Sixteen Tierces of Porter, dated March 22, 1798.

(A tierce was an old cask size, containing 32 gallons.)

Stout and porter were the main products of the brewery between 1920 and 1960. The earlier regular output of ale for the British troops stationed in Ireland came to an end in the 1920s following the withdrawal of the troops and the creation of a new Irish state.

The 1960s were a crucial time for the brewery. In 1962 it was bought by Canadian Breweries, which spent £1 million on modern facilities (including revolutionary fermentation and storage equipment) for brewing stout, lager and ale. By 1964 Carling Black Label lager was being brewed there, a move that helped the company to take advantage of the growing appetite for lager in Ireland. At that time it was widely predicted that stout would eventually disappear in the face of competition from lager, but the Irish did not give up their traditional drink so easily. Indeed, although lager continues to be a major seller and Carling Black Label remains a big earner for Beamish and Crawford, the 1990s have seen a rise in sales of stout, the only Irish beer product to show growth. In 1987 the huge Australian drinks company Elders IXL took over Canadian Breweries and hence Beamish and Crawford, a development that led to the appearance of Foster's lager on the Irish scene.

Up until 1960 the Beamish and Crawford brewery had operated much as it did in 1792, brewing with

Courtesy of Beamish and Crawford

The daily 'quarter-to-one' tasting session at Beamish and Crawford, Cork.
*Courtesy of Beamish and Crawford*

mash tuns and copper kettles which had been in regular use since 1865. Since then there has been a long process of modernisation, first under Canadian Breweries and later under Elders IXL, when high-gravity brewing was introduced.

Today's brewery is a fine example of brewing technology. Yet despite all the refinements of science, the checks and balances at every stage of the brewing process, the careful quality control in the laboratory, there is a final test that the company maintains it regards as the most important of all: the judgement of the human palate. So, after every brewing the seven brewers gather in the sampling room to sit in judgement on what has been produced, both before and after it is packed. The decision is reached by consensus: if a brew fails to receive the necessary level of approval it will be discarded.

All Irish brewers are proud of their products, of course, and Beamish and Crawford is as proud as any. The company began exporting Beamish stout to Britain in the mid-1980s and has been delighted by the results. Now, about 30 per cent of the company's output is exported in bulk shipments to Young's, Courage and Bass in Britain and distributed as kegged stout. Beamish is also available in France,

Courtesy of Beamish and Crawford

Spain and North America. The company emphasises that Beamish is the only Irish stout brewed exclusively in Ireland.

### DAYS THAT USED TO BE

There is a strong family tradition at both Cork breweries. It is quite common to find two and three generations of families working for the same company. At Beamish and Crawford, the remaining link with the Beamish family was severed only recently with the death of Richard Beamish, the great-great-grandson of the founder.

Courtesy of Beamish and Crawford

A pleasant ritual takes place at the Beamish brewery in Cork every Friday morning when pensioners gather in the sample room to meet their former workmates and take a glass or three at the company's expense. The combined experience of a typical group adds up to hundreds of years; the pensioners are a living encyclopaedia of the life and times of brewing in Cork.

Their memories are long: one old man recalls his father starting at the brewery as 'a barefoot lad of eleven' and completing sixty-four years of service; father and son worked for the brewery for more than one hundred years.

The pensioners express pride in their skills (which were once an essential part of the work of every brewery), especially after a few glasses of stout. A cooper remembers details of the craft of making and repairing barrels: always working by eye, never using a rule, never working under artificial light, explaining how a barrel would sometimes hold only 15 gallons instead of the required 16 and how the staves had to be precisely trimmed to create the necessary capacity. Another pensioner recalls a highly skilled job that has long since disappeared: that of the tapper who accompanied the delivery driver and whose job was to set up and prepare, or 'tap', the barrels. For many years stout was delivered to the publican in two barrels, one of which was a high pressure barrel and required special care in tapping. The stout served was

a mixture from both barrels.

All this ended in the early 1960s when a profound change in beer technology occurred with the phasing out of naturally conditioned products in wooden barrels and their replacement by bright, pasteurised products in metal kegs. The stout was delivered in a single barrel and served with the aid of pressure from a mixture of gases contained in a separate cylinder. These new methods were adopted by Ireland's stout brewers on the grounds that they gave the customer a better, more consistent pint. This view is now largely unchallenged, but opinion among those who knew the stout of the old days remains divided. Some accept that the modern version is better but others defend the old ways. They point to the fact that formerly the stout was conditioned naturally, then stored for ten days before leaving the brewery. A former Beamish employee remembers how carragheen moss was used for finings, and argues that something must have gone from the stout now that this plant, noted for its medicinal properties as well as being a culinary delicacy, is no longer used.

At this distance in time, it is impossible to adjudicate between the two sides, except to note that critics of modern stout do not allow their reservations to prevent them drinking the modern product – and with every appearance of enjoyment.

The Shandon steeple overlooking Murphy's brewery yard, Cork. Courtesy of Murphy Brewery Ireland

### MURPHY IS YOUR MAN

Murphy's stout has a light, sunny nature and slips down the throat with extraordinary ease. It is a companionable sort of drink, encouraging the exchange of civilised conversation so that one glass is inevitably followed by another and time wings by most agreeably. Its character is closer to Guinness than to its archrival Beamish, but it has a distinct personality that is very much its own. Some say it epitomises the spirit of Cork, that it is as beguiling as the people of the city – who have a natural taste for the good things of life.

The travel writer Eric Newby came across Murphy's while travelling in Ireland researching one of his many books. He gave his verdict after 'having absorbed two memorable pints of Murphy's stout':

> Brewed in Cork, Murphy's is different from Guinness, more velvety, and a taste for either, if over-indulged, can lead to smiles all round for the shareholders and for the consumer a dramatic change of profile and/or a visit to the bankruptcy court.

Mr Newby is clearly a man of excellent taste, but his general conclusions seem rather sweeping, especially when based on a quantity of Murphy's that, as any Cork man would confirm, is hardly enough to clear the dust of travel from the throat.

Splendid though it is as a drink in its own right, Murphy's reaches heavenly heights when married to another of Cork's attractions, the oyster. A pint of Murphy's and a half-dozen – better still, a dozen – of Cork's plump oysters at, say, the Oyster Tavern in the heart of the city is an experience as exquisite and

The Oyster Tavern

unforgettable as first hearing Verdi's *Requiem* or seeing the Casa d'Oro from the Grand Canal in Venice on a sunny spring day.

James Murphy and Co. Limited began in 1856 when four Murphy brothers set up in business in premises at Lady's Well that had formerly been a foundling hospital and had the kind of spacious buildings and access to a good water supply the new brewery would need. The name Lady's Well comes from a celebrated well, on the hill opposite the brewery, that is dedicated to the Virgin Mary and is believed to have miraculous properties. Pilgrimages are still made to the shrine each year in May.

The choice of site for the brewery proved fortunate, and within a few years, Lady's Well had become one of Cork's largest breweries. The Murphy brothers were described as follows by one commentator in 1890:

> These gentlemen applied themselves with energy and enterprise to the manufacture of an article, the reputation of which now extends far beyond the South of Ireland where the firm's stout and porter have been long and favourably known and where they command a very exclusive sale.

There are no secret ingredients in the stout, no special additives. The recipe is simple: roasted barley and malt, yeast, hops and water. The lighter taste may come from fewer hops being used than is the case with Murphy's rivals. The company believes the quality of Murphy's comes from the brewing methods used. The most stringent standards of quality control are maintained at every stage of the process.

Inside Murphy's brewery, Cork.
Courtesy of Murphy Brewery Ireland

The company claims it has the most modern brewery in Ireland, and it is true that when Heineken took over the company in 1983 a huge investment programme costing £35 million began, which resulted in a new brewery on the same site as the old plant. The technology is highly advanced: to the uninformed eye the new brewhouse seems to have more in common with space exploration than stout-brewing. Operatives manage all operations from a control station, computers store brewing recipes, control steam valves, measure levels of stores in silos and constantly monitor the brewing process. But the company insists that the skill of the brewers is every bit as important as technology. The human factor is crucial all along the line, right down to the vital matter of how the pint is dispensed to the customer in the bar or pub.

Courtesy of Murphy Brewery Ireland

The Murphy brewery was in the vanguard of developing gas systems for dispensing when the switch from wooden barrels to steel kegs took place in the 1960s. The change brought benefits, but the company was a little sorry that it had to abandon its popular advertising slogan 'Murphy's from the wood, that's good'. Murphy Brewery Ireland Limited now uses a mixture of 30 per cent carbon dioxide and 70 per cent nitrogen for dispensing stout, and a different gas mixture for dispensing Heineken lager. Gas makes dispensing the stout much easier than formerly, but the human element is still significant. Like Guinness, Murphy Brewery Ireland Limited places great emphasis on training bar staff to fill the glass up to one inch or so from the top, wait for twenty seconds or so and then top it up so that the creamy head rises proudly above the rim.

Murphy's – the world's first bottled draught stout.
Courtesy of Murphy Brewery Ireland

Murphy's is now well known far beyond Cork. Serious efforts at exporting to Britain began in 1986, but today only a small percentage of the stout brewed at the Lady's Well brewery is exported because Murphy's is brewed in Britain by Whitbread.

Murphy's brewery, Cork, in the nineteenth century.
Courtesy of Murphy Brewery Ireland

John Jameson
Heritage Centre,
Midleton, County
Cork

R. T. MILLS

# 7

## WHISKEY

## AND

## STOUT

### ON THE TOURIST TRAIL

*Knowledge is a rich storehouse . . .*

FRANCIS BACON

As whiskey and stout are among Ireland's greatest attractions for tourists, it is appropriate that there are a number of centres where visitors can learn more about them.

The John Jameson Heritage Centre was developed around the original buildings on the site of the former distillery of the Cork Distilleries Company at Midleton, 13 miles east of Cork city. The buildings had been left empty after the modern distilling complex on an adjoining site began operations in 1975, and in the nature of what is usually called 'progress' might well have been dismantled and put to some other use such as providing hardcore for roads. In this case, happily, the march of time was not so relentless as it often is and in 1990 an ambitious programme of restoration and refurbishment was launched to develop the 10-acre site as a tourist information centre.

The result, opened in 1992, was immediately successful, indicating a healthy interest on the part of tourists in either whiskey, or industrial archaeology, or both. Here visitors – principally from Ireland, Europe and the United States – can follow the story of how whiskey was made, in the authentic setting of a traditional distillery.

Pride of place in the John Jameson Heritage Centre goes to a magnificent pot still of burnished copper, the world's largest, with a capacity of 31,648 gallons. It was in use until 1975. Engineers played the part of today's scientists in the distilling industry of the past, using the latest technology of their day in the service of industry: this glowing copper still in which all the rivets were driven by hand is a fine example of the workmanship of the Dublin firm of Daniel Miller and Company.

R. T. MILLS

John Jameson Heritage Centre, Midleton, County Cork

Another great machine on show at the centre is a huge waterwheel made by Fairbairn in 1852. Made of cast iron, it has a diameter of 22 feet; the outer rim of the wheel is decorated with sheaves of barley cast in the iron, an indication that the makers knew the use to which the waterwheel would be put. This great wheel powered five pairs of millstones in the distillery, which were used to grind the barley and malt into the mix, called 'grist', that is soaked with hot water in the first part of the whiskey making process. Waterwheels were the main source of power employed in the distillery in the nineteenth century – in fact, this one, like the pot still, was still in use until 1975. Other machinery on display includes an original stationery steam engine and a horse-drawn, steam-powered fire engine. There is also an audiovisual show, craft shops and a large bar where the essential business of sampling takes place.

In Dublin, at the old Jameson distillery at Bow Street, is the Irish Whiskey Corner, a museum of the history of Irish whiskey which offers daily tours for visitors that include an audiovisual show and an opportunity to sample and compare whiskies from Ireland, Scotland and the United States.

Fire engine, John Jameson Heritage Centre, Midleton, County Cork.
Courtesy of Irish Distillers Group

Irish Whiskey Corner, Dublin.
Courtesy of Irish Distillers Group

Old Bushmills distillery, County
Antrim.
Courtesy of Old Bushmills distillery

Bushmills distillery in County Antrim also welcomes visitors, providing guided tours of the distillery with opportunities for buying souvenirs in the gift shops and plenty of scope for sampling.

Any lover of Guinness visiting Dublin should make time to see the Hop Store at the Guinness headquarters in St James's Gate. A museum of brewing has been created in a Victorian building originally used to store hops used in the brewing of Guinness. It is an absorbing collection of everything to do with brewing; among the items on view are a kieve built in 1878, a copper dating from 1836, a steam engine of 1888, and old wooden vats. There is a reconstruction of a traditional floor malting and a representation of a huge tun with a capacity of 288,000 gallons, in its day the largest fermenting vessel in the world. There is an audiovisual display on the history of Guinness, a selection of the famous Guinness advertising posters through the years, and a cooperage display which, with the help of models, recalls the skills of the coopers who made the wooden casks by hand. The transport museum includes a section devoted to the famous Guinness dray horses and to the narrow-gauge locomotives once used to transport raw materials around the brewery. Finally, there is a bar at which closer acquaintance with the product can be made.

Delivering Guinness , 1904.
Courtesy of Guinness Museum

8

# IRISH GLASS

A

## GREAT TRADITION

*Ramsey, Gatchell and Barcroft respectively inform their friends and the public that they have purchased the establishment of the Waterford Flint Glass manufactory from George and William Penrose and have opened a shop on the Quay in said concern where they intend to be supplied with an extensive assortment of plain and ornamental glassware and hope by their attention, moderate prices and the quality of their glass, to merit the approbation of their customers.*

WATERFORD CHRONICLE, DECEMBER 1799

A book dedicated to the drinks of Ireland could hardly ignore the contribution of Irish glass to the pleasures of drinking. No one would claim that Irish whiskey tastes better when drunk from crystal, but crystal certainly adds to the quality of the experience: the subtle, tawny highlights of the drink shimmer in the delicate patterns cut into the glass; there is something delightfully sensual in the feel of the cool, smooth surface against the lips and there is something comforting about the weight of the tumbler in the hand.

In fact, the making of Irish crystal, the distilling of Irish whiskey, and the brewing of Irish stout have quite a lot in common. All three processes have their roots in ancient traditions, use natural materials and

Potash, litharge and sand.
Courtesy of Terry Murphy Photography

Blowing crystal, *c.* 1800.
Courtesy of Waterford Crystal

depend upon human skills to achieve the finest results.

The raw materials of glass are sand, litharge and potash, which are transformed by fire into sparkling crystal. After being heated to 1,400 degrees centigrade for thirty-six hours, the molten crystal is ready for the centuries-old art of blowing, which is done with implements that have barely changed since the eighteenth century. The blower gathers the molten crystal on the end of the blowing iron, and the glowing material is shaped with a wooden block into the outline of the required item. He then blows through the rod to create the cavity inside the crystal. The operation requires great dexterity and coordination of hands, breath and strength. It is during this process that the wall thickness of the item being made is determined, a crucial factor influencing the depth of the patterns that will be cut into the crystal.

Blowing a large crystal gather.
Courtesy of Waterford Crystal

Glass making is very much a group effort. There is something almost balletic about the way the four-man teams work together around the furnace, each member of the team making a perfectly timed contribution to the assembly of each piece. Conditions around the furnace are very hot and it might seem appropriate that the men should quench their thirst with Irish stout, but because the work is so demanding, potentially dangerous, and requires such high levels of skill, the only drinks they allow themselves are strictly nonalcoholic.

Since the eighteenth century, Irish crystal has been famous for its deeply cut patterns, the inspiration for which often came from the Irish landscape, from flowers and trees, motifs that still adorn the Waterford Crystal made today. These patterns are cut into the surface of the crystal by diamond-tipped wheels or carborundum and sandstone, and always by hand. Before cutting begins, the uncut crystal called the 'blank' is marked with a geometric grid pattern of horizontal and vertical lines which guide the cutter as he applies the desired pattern. The design is cut strictly from memory. Teams of cutters work on each piece, the largest of which will take several days to complete.

County Waterford

Cutting the crystal.
Courtesy of Terry Murphy Photography

Extraordinary ability is required for the engraving process which, like the cutting, begins with an ink outline of the required motif, but this outline is drawn freehand onto the crystal by the engraver. The engraving is done with small copper wheels coated with an abrasive paste; very fine details can be achieved. A number of magnificent engraved pieces are made at Waterford, usually intended as trophies for the victors in various sporting competitions such as golf and tennis.

Waterford Crystal's Visitor Centre at Waterford has become a tourist attraction in its own right. Visitors from all over the world come to learn about the history of glass, to see the actual production areas and to marvel at the crystal gallery where some of the company's finest work is exhibited in a shimmering display of glasses, decanters, bowls, chandeliers and individual crystal sculptures. Among these is an actual-size violin valued at £20,000. After seeing a display of this kind, it is not surprising to learn that it takes an apprenticeship of eight years to become a master craftsman.

As with so much of Ireland's history, the story of

Engraving the crystal with a copper wheel .
Courtesy of Terry Murphy Photography

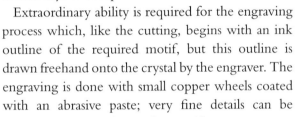

glass has been influenced by political as well as commercial considerations.

Glass has been made in Ireland since the Iron Age, principally for jewellery, and was often used in

Waterford sweetmeat dish,
*c.* 1830.
Courtesy of Terry Murphy Photography

preference to precious stones. It was much prized by the leaders of early Gaelic society for personal ornamentation, often in dark blue which was decorated with bright colours.

In medieval times, glass tableware was imported and was therefore expensive and little known, except in the wealthiest households. By the early 1600s, however, glass factories began to be set up in Ireland, especially where thick forests were on hand to provide wood to fuel the furnaces, as was the case in the Waterford area. Records exist of a factory in the south of County Waterford in 1618, and by the early eighteenth century, glass making in Ireland was clearly well established. A Waterford manufacturer advertised in 1729 that he was able to supply the latest crystal drinking glasses, and Irish glass makers soon won both a reputation for the quality of their work and a thriving market in London and Dublin.

Unfortunately, this flourishing industry was hit by what can only be called an act of typical chauvinism by the Westminster government of the day when it decreed in 1746 that the export of glass from Ireland was prohibited and that only glass from England was allowed to be imported into Ireland. The Irish industry was crippled by these restrictions for several decades and only recovered when the Westminster government, predictable only in its perversity, saddled the English glass industry with heavy additional taxation. In 1777 the duty on glass in England was doubled, but Irish glass was exempted and restrictions on the export of glass from Ireland were ended. Freed from duty, the Irish manu-facturers were able to use the properties of lead glass to the full, blowing it thick and cutting deep patterns into the crystals that caught reflections of light more effectively than thinner glass. When free trade followed in the late eighteenth century, there was a

The factory at Ballytruckle,
Waterford, 1948.
Courtesy of Terry Murphy Photography

great resurgence in the Irish glass industry, which entered its most creative and exuberant phase.

The firm of Waterford Crystal, founded in 1783 in the city of Waterford, was part of this fertile period in which Irish craftsmanship in glass reached heights of invention in design and quality that continue to inspire modern designers. A sequence of increasingly elaborate motifs – diamonds, swags, flutes – was created, cut deeply into the glass, catching the play of light. These pieces, especially those from Waterford, are valuable and greatly prized by modern collectors – but it has often been pointed out that more glass has been identified as Waterford than was ever made in the whole of Ireland.

Despite its reputation and success, the Waterford factory closed in 1851, a victim of heavy taxation following the Union of 1801. By a strange irony, 1851 was the year of the Great Exhibition at the Crystal Palace in London, to which the company sent a splendid exhibit. The closure was a crushing blow to the Irish glass industry, which ceased to exist soon afterwards.

The story might well have ended there, but the memory of Irish crystal remained strong because so many fine examples survived. At regular intervals there was talk that Ireland had a patriotic duty to revive its famous industry but it was not until 1947 that a small glass factory was opened at Ballytruckle, a suburb of Waterford, little more than a mile or so from the original Waterford Crystal factory.

The Waterford exhibit at Crystal Palace, 1851.
Courtesy of Terry Murphy Photography

Waterford bowl, *c.* 1950.
Courtesy of Terry Murphy Photography

Expert blowers and cutters from Europe provided the skills for the new factory and trained local apprentices. The inspiration, however, was the great Waterford tradition of the past, and the brilliant chief designer of Waterford Crystal at the time, Miroslav Havel, used the collections in the National Museum of Ireland as a springboard for his creations. The traditional, deeply incised cutting patterns of the old Waterford Crystal became the design basis for the new company's products. The company's success throughout the world has been phenomenal, particularly in the United States, where it has become a byword for Irish craft skills.

## 9

### CHARGE YOUR GLASSES

In addition to 'Sláinte', Irish for 'Good health to you', which is heard daily in every pub in Ireland, there are many other Irish toasts. Most of these date from the eighteenth century, although the word 'toast' is thought to have originated in the sixteenth century.

There are a few simple rules to observe. The glass for the toast is customarily raised in the right hand and it is held straight out from the shoulder. This is done to show the toaster comes in friendship, and it dates from the time when a weapon might be concealed in the right hand or in clothing. It is traditional to clink glasses after the toast has been proposed but before it has been drunk. This is said to be linked to the ancient belief that a noise – the ringing of a bell or the clinking of glass – frightens away evil spirits.

Here are some toasts to share with friends.

DERMOT DONOHUE

## BIRTHDAY TOASTS

May you live 100 years
But with an extra year to repent.

May you die in bed aged 100 years
Shot by a jealous husband.

May you live as long as you want
And never want as long as you live.

## DINNER PARTY TOASTS

May the roof above us never fall in
And may we friends gathered below it never fall
    out.

Here's a health to thine and thee
Not forgetting mine and me
When thine and thee next meet mine and me
May mine and me have as much welcome for
    thine and thee
As thine and thee have had for mine and me
    tonight.

## GOOD HEALTH TOAST

May your doctor never earn a penny out of you
May your heart never give out
May the ten toes of your feet steer you clear of
    all misfortune
And before you're much older
May you hear much better toasts than this.

A TOAST FOR THE FARMER

May the frost never afflict your spuds
May the outside leaves of your cabbage always
    be free from worm
May the crows never pick at your haystack
And may your ass always be in foal.

A TOAST GIVING GOOD WISHES

May you be poor in misfortune
Rich in blessings
Slow to make enemies
Quick to make friends
But rich or poor
Quick or slow
May you know nothing but happiness
From this day forth.

Courtesy of Guinness Museum

A TOAST FOR A BACHELOR

May you have prettier legs than your own under
    the table
Before the new spuds are up.

Many of these toasts will be heard in Irish pubs where most Irish drinking is done and where the Irish drinks of whiskey and stout dominate. There is a rather curious difference between whiskey drinking in Ireland and in Britain. More than 60 per cent of the whiskey drunk in Ireland is bought in bars and pubs – in Britain the situation is completely different with 80 per cent bought by the bottle for drinking at home.

There are no rules about how Irish whiskey should be drunk. Some take it with ice, on the rocks, some with mixers, but the finest whiskies such as Black Bush and Jameson 1780 should be drunk undiluted. The addition of water is also very much a matter of personal choice, as is indicated by the old Irish saying 'You must never steal another man's wife and you must never water another man's whiskey.'

Perhaps the most famous combination of Irish drinks is Irish coffee, which is Irish whiskey with coffee and cream. This fairly recent invention is a development of the old practice of adding whiskey to tea, which has been common in Ireland ever since tea drinking became popular in the eighteenth century. Irish coffee was the creation of Joe Sheridan, chief barman at Shannon Airport just after the Second World War, who transformed the tea-and-whiskey combination to appeal to the tastes of visiting Americans who made up most of the travellers through Shannon at that time. Sheridan substituted coffee for tea, added sugar, and topped it with a layer of fresh, lightly whipped Irish cream. Finally, he served it in a glass rather than a cup to show off the contrast between the black coffee and the white cream. He never served it with a spoon or straw, instead encouraging customers to drink the hot coffee and whiskey mixture through the cold cream.

### JOE SHERIDAN'S AUTHENTIC RECIPE FOR IRISH COFFEE

Into a stemmed glass, put two teaspoonfuls of sugar, preferably brown; add one third by volume Irish whiskey and two thirds really hot, really strong black coffee, preferably fresh, not instant. The glass should be filled with this mixture to within half an inch (1 centimetre) of the brim. Stir well to ensure all the sugar is dissolved, and then, without stirring, carefully float over the back of a spoon a collar of lightly whipped cream, so that the cream floats on top of the coffee and whiskey.

DERMOTT DUNBAR

# BIBLIOGRAPHY

Among the many books, pamphlets, newspapers and magazines that have contributed in some measure to this work I should like to pay special tribute to the following:

Arthur Barnard, THE WHISKY DISTILLERS OF THE UNITED KINGDOM, published in 1887 and in 1967 by David and Charles

J.C. Beckett, THE MAKING OF MODERN IRELAND, Faber and Faber, 1966

Brian Harrison, DRINK AND THE VICTORIAN: THE TEMPERANCE QUESTION IN ENGLAND 1815–72, Faber and Faber, 1971

Maurice Healey, STAY ME WITH FLAGONS, Michael Joseph, 1940

Alf McCreary, SPIRIT OF THE AGE, Old Bushmills Distillery Company, 1983

Malachy Magee, 1,000 YEARS OF IRISH WHISKEY, O'Brien Press, 1980

James Ross, WHISKY, Routledge and Kegan Paul, 1970

George Saintsbury, NOTES ON A CELLAR BOOK, Macmillan, 1920

R.N. Salaman, THE HISTORY AND SOCIAL INFLUENCE OF THE POTATO, Cambridge University Press, 1949

Katherine Scherman, THE FLOWERING OF IRELAND, Gollancz, 1981

Cecil Woodham-Smith, THE GREAT HUNGER, Hamish Hamilton, 1962

Arthur Young, A TOUR IN IRELAND, edited by Constantia Maxwell, Cambridge University Press, 1925, and Blackstaff Press, 1983